I0816240

HELLO KITTY® AND FRIENDS
THE COOKBOOK

HELLO KITTY® AND FRIENDS
THE COOKBOOK

Supercute Recipes for Fun and Friendship

JENN FUJIKAWA

RUNNING PRESS
PHILADELPHIA

Running Press
Hachette Book Group
1290 Avenue of the Americas, New York, NY 10104
www.runningpress.com
@Running_Press

First Edition: October 2025

Published by Running Press, an imprint of Hachette Book Group, Inc.
The Running Press name and logo are trademarks of Hachette Book Group, Inc.

The Hachette Speakers Bureau provides a wide range of authors for speaking events. To find out more, go to www.hachettespeakersbureau.com or email HachetteSpeakers@hbgusa.com.

Running Press books may be purchased in bulk for business, educational, or promotional use. For more information, please contact your local bookseller or the Hachette Book Group Special Markets Department at Special.Markets@hbgusa.com.

The publisher is not responsible for websites (or their content) that are not owned by the publisher.

Print book cover and interior design by Mary Boyer
Illustrations by Le Delicatessen

Library of Congress Cataloging-in-Publication Data
Names: Fujikawa, Jenn author
Title: Hello Kitty and friends: the cookbook: supercute recipes for fun and friendship/Jenn Fujikawa.
Description: First edition. | Philadelphia: Running Press, 2025. | Includes index. |
Summary: "Inspired by the global phenomenon Hello Kitty, this official cookbook will appeal to Hello Kitty and Friends' large and passionate fan base, offering fun and delicious recipes from classic dishes to comfort meals"—Provided by publisher.
Identifiers: LCCN 2025005168 (print) | LCCN 2025005169 (ebook) |
ISBN 9798894140803 hardcover | ISBN 9798894140988 epub
Subjects: LCSH: Cooking | Hello Kitty (Fictitious character)—Miscellanea |
LCGFT: Cookbooks
Classification: LCC TX714.F835 2025 (print) | LCC TX714 (ebook) |
DDC 641.5—dc23/eng/20250227
LC record available at https://lccn.loc.gov/2025005168
LC ebook record available at https://lccn.loc.gov/2025005169

ISBNs: 979-8-89414-080-3 (hardcover), 979-8-89414-098-8 (ebook)

Printed in China

APS

10 9 8 7 6 5 4 3 2 1

CONTENTS

INTRODUCTION

In the supercute world of Hello Kitty and her friends, Hello Kitty's friends include sweet and friendly Keroppi, the mischievous Badtz-maru, the curious Chococat, the very refined penguin Tuxedosam, My Melody the supportive and caring friend, Pochacco the playful pup, the creative LittleTwinStars, Kiki and Lala, the cheeky but charming Kuromi, the laid-back dog Pompompurin, humorous and romantic Hangyodon, and the kind-hearted puppy Cinnamoroll.

With this cookbook, you can explore the world of Hello Kitty and her friends. Each character's distinctive personality makes them unique. Their hobbies and pastimes influence their tastes and particular palates. It's these characteristics that bring the best buddies together to enjoy each other's company and share their favorite eats.

Hello Kitty is a little girl with a big heart who loves her friends and family. Born in London, England, her sister, Mimmy, is her closest friend. Apples are a big part of Hello Kitty's life. Not only is she five apples tall, but she weighs as much as three apples. And although she loves baking cookies, her mama's apple pie is her favorite thing to eat (see page 73).

A triplet, Keroppi has a sister, Pikki, and a brother named Koroppi. He gets his love of good food from his mother who runs a restaurant on the edge of Donut Pond, where they live. She makes many good things to eat but Keroppi's favorite are the rice balls she makes (see page 40). They're great after a long day of playing baseball and boomerang with friends.

Badtz-maru lives in Gorgeoustown with his mother and pinball-playing father. An attention seeker, he loves the stares he gets as he walks his pet alligator, Pochi. He was born on Oahu in Hawaii, so he likes to indulge in fresh fish. He does have pretty high-end tastes though, as his favorite food to eat is expensive sushi in Ginza (see page 49). He's a lot of fun, if not a little mischievous.

Chococat is all about chocolate. He gets his name from his chocolate-colored nose, and he lives in Choco-choco House. That's a lot of chocolate. It's such a big part of his life that one of his favorite hobbies is eating sweet candies and desserts—especially chocolate candy and a chocolate chip cookie he enjoys with a big glass of milk (see page 72).

An elegant fella with amazing fashion sense, Tuxedosam owns 365 bow ties, one for every day of the year. He was born on Tuxedo Island in Antarctica but studied abroad and lives in England, which is most likely where he developed his refined palate for the finer things, like his favorite meal, shrimp coquille, which is served in a very fancy seashell (see page 54).

An iconic pink hood can mean only one thing: My Melody. Her wearable accessory was a gift from her beloved grandmother. My Melody's best friend is Hello Kitty, and they both love to have fun and enjoy baking. Cooking and being in the kitchen with her mom is her happy place, and while My Melody likes to bake cookies with her mother, when it comes to eating, she can't resist a slice of almond pound cake (see page 77).

If there's a playful pup around, it must be Pochacco. This sporty pal loves being outdoors. Athletic and amicable, he can also be a little bit clumsy. His height is the equivalent of four large cups of his favorite food, banana ice cream (see page 71). His weight is the equivalent of three Fuwafuwa Town carrots. Coincidentally, his hometown, Fuwafuwa Town, is filled with carrot fields.

Kiki and Lala, the LittleTwinStars, were born on the Omoiyari Star and traveled to Earth for more adventures. Kiki's star on his back allows him to fly while Lala's star wand makes snacks appear, which can be super helpful since she's a great cook. Her skills in the kitchen are appreciated by her brother, who loves to eat the pancakes she makes (see page 15).

Cheeky and charming, Kuromi is always in style! Her tomboy style and mischievous attitude set her apart from the rest. Her characteristic black and pink hood are her charm points. That's not the only unique thing about Kuromi—while most characters go for sweets, her favorite foods range from pickled onions to shallots.

The super laid-back Pompompurin is a golden retriever who is as squishy as the foods he loves to eat. He loves making friends and doing "purin aerobics" so he can get bigger and bouncier. Going out with his friends keeps him happy, and so does eating. His favorite foods include milk, soft foods, and his mom's special milk pudding (see page 83).

An aspiring comedian, Hangyodon is a lonely romantic at heart. He likes to eat shrimp crackers and hot pot. But in the end, he'd really like to have someone to share those things with him.

Flying down from the sky with his big floppy ears, Cinnamoroll landed at the Cinnamoroll Cafe and stayed permanently. So named after his small tail that curls up like a cinnamon roll, he fits right in. He loves dancing like his favorite pop idols, napping, and enjoying a yummy treat—which is a good thing since his favorite food is his namesake, the cinnamon muffins at the cafe (see page 6).

For Hello Kitty and her friends, their common interests involve having fun and appreciating good food. Cooking with companions can bring a sense of togetherness. It's a great way to find out how to use new-to-you ingredients and learn about different cultures.

In this cookbook, whether it's full meals of breakfast, lunch, and dinner or light drinks and desserts, every friend is represented. Specialty flavors are distinctive to their upbringing, location, and hobbies. From flowers and bow accessories to foods from their hometown, every dish puts a character's attributes front and center, and each recipe reflects individuality and personal taste.

Food brings people together. And being able to share interesting conversation over a great meal is the best way to forge lifelong bonds. Learning from each other, exploring and expanding your interests, and adding a touch of supercute fun will make spending time together even more special. The delicious connection between Hello Kitty and her friends is the happiness that food brings, and a celebration of friendship!

GF	Gluten Free
V	Vegetarian
V+	Vegan
-	N/A

CHAPTER ONE

Charming Breakfasts

Breakfast is said to be the most important meal of the day. If you're like Hello Kitty and her friends, you'll want something significant, filling, and full of flavor to keep you going until lunch. Pochacco needs a big meal to keep up his energy, while Pompompurin might get up for a quick bite, only to go back for a second morning nap. Whatever they start their morning with sets the tone for the rest of the day.

Pancakes are often the first thing that comes to mind when you think of breakfast. A big stack of steaming flapjacks will instantly bring a smile to anyone's face. LittleTwinStars put a fun twist on traditional pancakes, because what's a morning meal without a touch of star magic? Lala's Strawberry Pancakes (page 15) are made special by adding strawberries to both the batter and topping.

Hello Kitty and her friends are always on the go and Chococat Breakfast Bars (page 12) and Pompompurin Yogurt Parfait (page 20) are great meals for friends who have a full day of activities. Quick to grab but high on energy, these morning meals will have you on your way in no time. Whether it's rushing to school or work, working hard to play hard requires a lot of discipline, and these easy meals will help keep up your spirits.

For those who lack a sweet tooth, breakfast comes in many forms and doesn't always have to lean to the sweet variety. A hearty bowl of fish and rice is the ideal start to the day for someone like Hangyodon. In Japan, a morning meal can consist of savory foods like Hangyodon Salmon Chazuke (page 11). Hot green tea poured over fish and rice is just what you need for a full belly in the morning.

Any of these eats is a great choice to kick off your day. Savory or sweet, a good breakfast can inspire your mood. Fill up in the morning to push away the morning grumpiness and welcome what's to come. Whether you're heading to work, school, or a day off to hang out at Donut Pond, you'll be fully prepared to take on whatever comes your way.

Hello Kitty Lemon Scones

MAKES
8
SERVINGS

Born in London, England, Hello Kitty is used to enjoying teatime. A nice cup of tea and some dainty finger sandwiches paired with soft, aromatic scones is a daily ritual that can make any day better. These scones are full of citrusy lemon flavor and topped with a sweet strawberry bite, shaped into a perfect tiny bow. Served for breakfast, these beautiful bites make a lovely teatime treat for Hello Kitty to share with her sister, Mimmy.

2½ cups all-purpose flour, plus more for dusting

¼ cup granulated sugar

3 tablespoons grated lemon zest

1 tablespoon baking powder

¼ teaspoon kosher salt

6 tablespoons unsalted butter, cold and cubed

½ cup whole milk

¼ cup fresh lemon juice

1 large egg, beaten

4 or 5 fresh strawberries, hulled

¼ cup heavy cream

In a large bowl whisk the flour, sugar, lemon zest, baking powder, and salt to combine.

With a pastry cutter, cut the butter into the flour mixture until it resembles coarse crumbs.

Stir in the milk, lemon juice, and egg until just combined. Refrigerate the dough for 15 minutes.

Preheat the oven to 400°F. Line a baking sheet with parchment paper.

Lightly dust your work surface with flour and place the dough on it. Pat the dough into a 1-inch thickness. Use a 2-inch round cutter to cut out dough rounds and place them on the prepared baking sheet 2 inches apart.

Slice the strawberries from top to bottom and place two pieces on top of each scone, small ends together, to create a bow tie. Press the strawberries into the scones. Use a pastry brush to brush each scone with heavy cream.

Bake until lightly brown, 15 to 17 minutes. Transfer to a wire rack to cool.

Continues on next page

Keroppi Avocado Toast

MAKES
1
SERVING

Sports are a big part of Keroppi's life and one of his favorite pastimes is to enjoy a day of baseball around Donut Pond. A day full of outdoor play can be exhausting, so it's always best to eat a well-rounded breakfast to get ready for his adventures. Avocado toast provides nutrients and energy required for a day of fun and games with friends. It tastes even better when Keroppi's own sweet avocado face is smiling back.

1 slice white bread
1 tablespoon olive oil
1 garlic clove, peeled
½ large avocado
2 teaspoons fresh lime juice
¼ teaspoon kosher salt
⅛ teaspoon ground black pepper
1 hard-boiled egg, peeled and sliced
1 small slice ham
1 small piece nori

Brush one side of the bread with the olive oil. In a small skillet over medium heat, cook the bread, oil-side down, until lightly toasted, about 1 minute. Remove the bread from the pan and rub the toasted side with the garlic clove. Set aside.

Use a spoon to scoop the avocado into a small bowl and add the lime juice, salt, and pepper. Use a fork to mash the avocado until the ingredients are just combined. Spread the avocado mixture onto the toast, forming a rounded shape.

Place two white slices of hard-boiled egg on the avocado for the eyes.

Cut out two small round circles of ham and place them as the cheeks.

Finally, cut and place the nori to form the pupils of the eyes and the mouth. Serve immediately.

Cafe Cinnamon Cinnamoroll Muffins

MAKES
12
SERVINGS

Cafe Cinnamon serves many special dishes, but it's the most fragrant ones that keep customers coming back for more. Waiting for these to bake can feel tedious when you get a whiff of that sweet, sugary goodness, but Cinnamoroll's cuddles will help pass the time. Straight out of the oven, these muffins are hard to resist. Warm and deliciously sweet-scented, the unforgettable combination of cinnamon and sugar makes any morning even more magical.

FOR THE MUFFINS

2 cups all-purpose flour

½ cup packed light brown sugar

½ cup granulated sugar

2 teaspoons baking powder

1½ teaspoons ground cinnamon

½ teaspoon ground nutmeg

¼ teaspoon ground cloves

¼ teaspoon kosher salt

1 cup horchata

¼ cup vegetable oil

1 large egg, lightly beaten

1 teaspoon vanilla extract

FOR THE CRUMB TOPPING

⅓ cup all-purpose flour

¼ cup packed light brown sugar

½ teaspoon ground cinnamon

2 tablespoons unsalted butter, cold and diced

Preheat the oven to 375°F. Line a standard muffin tin with liners. Set aside.

To make the muffins: In a large bowl, whisk the flour, brown sugar, granulated sugar, baking powder, cinnamon, nutmeg, cloves, and salt to combine. Make a well in the center of the dry ingredients.

Pour in the horchata, oil, egg, and vanilla and stir until just combined. Spoon the batter into the prepared wells, dividing it evenly.

To make the crumb topping: In a small bowl, stir together the flour, brown sugar, and cinnamon.

With a fork, work the cold butter into the mixture until crumbly. Sprinkle each muffin with some of the crumb topping, dividing it evenly.

Bake for 15 to 17 minutes, or until an inserted toothpick comes out clean. Transfer to a wire rack to cool for 2 to 3 minutes before serving.

Breakfast muffins are a great start to the day; they pair well with coffee, tea, or juice and are easily portable. Cinnamoroll knows how good cinnamon is—it's a great base flavor to start off any sweet muffin. Try adding ingredients to the batter to elevate this recipe—crunchy walnuts, some chopped dried mango, or a dash of nutritional yeast, for good measure. The add-ins can make these muffins feel like a hearty morning meal.

Badtz-maru Smoothie Bowl

Who doesn't love a morning stroll? Badtz-maru likes to take his pet alligator, Pochi, for a walk in the morning. But, before that happens, he needs to wake up and get a little nourishment into his stomach to start the day. There's nothing quite as fortifying as a substantial smoothie in a bowl in the morning. It's just like eating a frosty bowl of fruit, which makes getting out of bed a lot easier.

FOR THE SMOOTHIE BOWL

2 cups frozen cubed peeled mango

1 banana, peeled and sliced

1 tablespoon fresh lemon juice

½ cup oat milk

FOR THE TOPPING

1 small banana, sliced

¼ cup fresh blueberries

2 or 3 fresh blackberries

1 tablespoon chia seeds

1 tablespoon shredded coconut

To make the smoothie bowl: In a blender, combine the mango, banana, lemon juice, and oat milk. Blend until smooth. Pour into a bowl.

To finish: Top the smoothie bowl with banana slices, blueberries, and blackberries. Sprinkle with the chia seeds and coconut to serve.

Badtz-maru was born on Oahu in Hawaii, thus his love of tropical fruits. The best thing about this smoothie bowl is that you can change it up with any ingredients you have on hand. Try strawberries, which are so versatile and make any meal sweeter. Berry lovers will tell you the redder the better. Keep that in mind when choosing your strawberries. Add a touch of bright color to your bowl with diced kiwi. Did you know you can eat the kiwi, peel and all? Try it, it's good for you! However you decide to personalize your smoothie bowl ingredients, take a page out of Badtz-maru's book and select your flavors with gusto!

Pochacco Soufflé Pancakes

MAKES
6
SERVINGS

Pochacco is a curious little guy who has a big animated and active personality. So, of course, his version of breakfast is unique. These Japanese soufflé pancakes are melt-in-your-mouth delicious and a fun alternative to a standard breakfast flap-jack. Soft and fluffy, they dance happily on your plate, making every morning a little brighter. Just like Pochacco's bouncy attitude, these interactive cakes will put a smile on your face so you can bounce into your day.

FOR THE PANCAKES

4 large eggs, separated

3 tablespoons whole milk

1 teaspoon vanilla extract

½ cup cake flour

1 teaspoon baking powder

¼ teaspoon ground nutmeg

¼ teaspoon kosher salt

¼ cup granulated sugar

2 tablespoons vegetable oil

4 tablespoons water

FOR SERVING

1 cup frozen whipped topping, defrosted

Fresh fruit, for serving

To make the pancakes: In a large bowl, whisk the egg yolks, milk, and vanilla until frothy, 1 to 2 minutes. Stir in the flour, baking powder, nutmeg, and salt until just combined. Set aside.

In a large, chilled bowl with a handheld mixer, whip the egg whites on medium speed until frothy, 1 to 2 minutes.

One tablespoonful at a time, add the sugar. Whip on high speed until stiff peaks form, 5 to 6 minutes. Gently fold the egg whites into the egg yolk mixture until just combined. Set aside.

Grease a large skillet with the oil, using a paper towel to spread it around, then wipe out the excess. Heat the skillet over low heat.

Transfer the batter into a piping bag. Pipe out three 2½-inch diameter pancakes, ¼ cup of batter each. Add 1 tablespoon of water to the skillet, cover, and cook for 2 minutes.

Continues on next page

Remove the lid and add a second layer of batter onto each pancake, another ¼ cup. Replace the lid and cook until golden brown on the bottom, 4 minutes. Carefully flip each pancake.

Add another tablespoon of water to the pan, re-cover, and cook until the pancakes are dry, 4 minutes. Transfer the pancakes to a serving plate.

Repeat with the remaining batter and water.

To serve: Add a scoop of whipped topping onto the pancakes. Serve with fresh fruit.

Hangyodon Salmon Chazuke

MAKES
1
SERVING

Hangyodon can happily eat seafood for three meals a day. Lunch is obvious, dinner a must, and, yes, even brunch gets the briny sea treatment. This traditional Japanese meal of fish and rice is topped with hot tea and is so warm and comforting you'll almost wonder if going back to bed is a better option. The protein will comfortably ease you into a fresh start to your morning. Once you've had your fill, the day is yours to do as you please.

FOR THE SALMON

- 1 (4-ounce) salmon fillet
- 1 tablespoon mirin
- ¼ teaspoon kosher salt

FOR THE CHAZUKE

- ¾ cup cooked short-grain rice, hot
- 1 cup brewed green tea, hot
- 1 tablespoon shredded nori
- 1 tablespoon pickled radish
- 1 teaspoon furikake rice seasoning

To make the salmon: Place the salmon fillet in a shallow dish and pour the mirin over it. Sprinkle with salt. Cover with plastic wrap and refrigerate for 2 hours.

When ready to cook, preheat the boiler and line a baking sheet with parchment paper.

Transfer the fish to the prepared baking sheet. Broil until lightly charred, 5 to 6 minutes. Let cool slightly, then flake the fish with a fork. Set aside.

To make the chazuke: Add the hot rice into a medium bowl. Top with the flaked salmon. Pour over the hot tea.

Garnish with nori, pickled radish, and furikake to serve.

Chococat Breakfast Bars

MAKES **8** SERVINGS

Chococat has places to go and people to see. Thanks to his ultrasensitive "antenna" whiskers, he is always up on the latest news, so he needs to get up and out in the morning. Filled with delicious peanut butter and oats, plus a bite of cranberry, you'll also find mini chocolate chips, an ode to Chococat's lil' chocolate nose, in these breakfast bars. These energizing bars are a big help so he can head out for the day and find out all the information to relay to his friends.

- **¼ cup packed light brown sugar**
- **¼ cup honey**
- **4 tablespoons unsalted butter**
- **2 tablespoons peanut butter**
- **½ teaspoon vanilla extract**
- **½ teaspoon ground cinnamon**
- **¼ teaspoon kosher salt**
- **1½ cups whole rolled oats**
- **1 cup oat cereal**
- **¼ cup mini semisweet chocolate chips**
- **¼ cup dried cranberries**

Line an 8 by 8-inch pan with parchment paper and grease the parchment with nonstick cooking spray. Set aside.

In a small saucepan over medium heat, combine the brown sugar, honey, butter, and peanut butter. Cook until the mixture starts to simmer, 1 minute. Remove from the heat.

Stir in the vanilla, cinnamon, and salt.

In a large bowl, combine the rolled oats, cereal, and brown sugar–butter mixture and toss to coat. Let cool slightly.

Fold in the chocolate chips and cranberries. Press the mixture into the prepared pan. Refrigerate for 2 hours.

Cut into bars to serve.

Chococat's penchant for chocolate is the inspiration for these breakfast bars, but you can easily change it up and put together other variations with new and exciting ingredients. Instead of chocolate chips and cranberries, try pepitas and yogurt chips. Choose some components based on your friends' interests. Chococat's buddy, Marshmallow—short for his full name, Mashumaromitainafuwafuwanyanko—is inspiration for another great ingredient to try in this breakfast bar, because marshmallows are sweet, just like friends. Be as adventurous as Chococat and try new things; you might find some exciting favorite flavors to try.

My Melody Egg Flowers

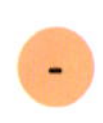

MAKES 1 SERVING

My Melody is a style icon. Her pink hood was made by her grandmother and is stylish all on its own, but it's the pretty flower adornment on the right side of her hood that brings the whole outfit together. This decorative accent is more than a statement—it's a breakfast inspiration. These egg flowers are fluffy, savory, and easy to make. Like little edible morning clouds, this savory dish is a light and airy start to the day.

FOR THE TOAST

2 slices brioche

1 tablespoon unsalted butter

2 thin slices ham

FOR THE EGGS

2 large eggs

⅛ teaspoon kosher salt

Dash of ground white pepper

Butter the brioche. Place the ham on top and lightly toast in a toaster oven. Set aside.

Preheat the oven to 450°F. Line a baking sheet with parchment paper.

To make the eggs: Separate the eggs, placing the whites in a large bowl. Set aside the yolks, keeping them intact.

Use a handheld mixer to beat the egg whites on medium speed until stiff peaks form. Use a rubber spatula to fold in the salt and white pepper.

Spoon the whipped whites into two separate mounds on the prepared baking sheet. With the back of a spoon, create an indentation in the center of each mound.

Bake until lightly set, 2 minutes.

Gently pour one of the reserved egg yolks into each indentation. Return to the oven and bake until the edges of the yolks are just set, 3 minutes.

Carefully place one egg on each ham-topped toast. Serve immediately.

Lala's Strawberry Pancakes

Lala loves being in the kitchen; it's her favorite place to be. While her brother, Kiki, is out star fishing, Lala can get creative and make magic with a variety of ingredients and unique flavors. One of Kiki's favorite meals is Lala's special pancakes. These fluffy flapjacks have fresh, ripe strawberries swirled throughout the batter, giving each bite a pop of fresh fruit flavor. Served with a healthy spoonful of cream cheese frosting, it's a picture-perfect breakfast for sharing.

FOR THE TOPPING

8 ounces cream cheese, at room temperature

¼ cup powdered sugar

3 tablespoons heavy cream

1 cup fresh strawberries, hulled and sliced

FOR THE PANCAKES

1 cup fresh strawberries, hulled and diced, divided

1 teaspoon fresh lemon juice

1 tablespoon packed light brown sugar

2 cups all-purpose flour

2 tablespoons granulated sugar

1 tablespoon baking powder

¼ teaspoon kosher salt

1½ cups whole milk

2 large eggs, lightly beaten

½ teaspoon vanilla extract

2 tablespoons unsalted butter, melted

To make the topping: In a medium bowl, combine the cream cheese, powdered sugar, and heavy cream. Use a hand mixer or a wooden spoon to mix until smooth. Transfer the frosting to a piping bag and refrigerate until ready to use.

To make the pancakes: In a small bowl, combine ½ cup of the diced strawberries, the lemon juice, and brown sugar. Use an immersion blender to blend until smooth, 3 to 4 minutes. Set aside.

In a large bowl, whisk the flour, granulated sugar, baking powder, and salt to combine. Make a well in the center of the dry ingredients.

Pour in the blended strawberry mixture, milk, eggs, and vanilla and stir until just combined. Stir in the remaining ½ cup diced strawberries and melted butter.

Continues on next page

Heat a large nonstick skillet over medium heat. Pour ⅓ cup of the batter, per pancake, into the skillet. Cook until bubbles start to form and pop, 2 to 3 minutes.

Flip the pancakes and cook until lightly browned, 1 minute. Transfer to plates and repeat with the remaining batter.

Pipe a dollop of the cream cheese frosting onto the pancakes and add sliced strawberries to serve.

Kuromi Chocolate Chip Pumpkin Waffles

Born in October, Kuromi is all about cutesy with a side of spooky, so naturally she also has a taste for all things pumpkin, and it just makes sense to incorporate it into a perfect fall breakfast dish. Mochiko gives these waffles a toothsome chew and the blend of spices elevates the flavors to peak comfort. Pumpkin is the punch of flavor that makes everything better while the chocolate chips take these waffles to the next level. Their distinct flavor and sweet taste are just as unique as Kuromi herself.

1 cup all-purpose flour

1 cup mochiko flour

3 tablespoons packed light brown sugar

2 teaspoons baking powder

½ teaspoon ground cinnamon

¼ teaspoon ground nutmeg

¼ teaspoon kosher salt

1½ cups whole milk

½ cup pumpkin puree

1 large egg, lightly beaten

1 teaspoon vanilla extract

1 tablespoon unsalted butter, melted

¾ cup chocolate chips

1 cup whipped cream, to serve

½ cup maple syrup, to serve

Preheat a waffle maker according to the manufacturer's instructions.

In a large bowl, whisk the all-purpose flour, mochiko, brown sugar, baking powder, cinnamon, nutmeg, and salt to combine. Make a well in the center of the dry ingredients.

Add the milk, pumpkin, egg, and vanilla and stir until just combined.

Stir in the melted butter. Fold in the chocolate chips.

Pour ½ cup of the batter into the waffle maker. Cook until golden brown (the time will vary depending on your waffle maker). Repeat with the remaining batter.

Serve with whipped cream and maple syrup.

Tuxedosam Tuxedo Eggs

MAKES **12** SERVINGS

Tuxedosam is a dapper fella and that aesthetic applies to everything in his life—from his outfit to his breakfast. His penchant for style is the inspiration for this unique morning repast. A boiled egg is fine on its own, but adding a little flair takes the egg from basic to enchanting. The eggs' coloring is an ode to Tuxedosam's fetching blue hue and his attire is represented by a tiny bell pepper bow tie. Very distinguished.

6 large eggs

4 cups water

3 drops blue food coloring

3 tablespoons Japanese mayonnaise

1 tablespoon diced gherkins

2 teaspoons yellow mustard

¼ teaspoon Old Bay seasoning

¼ teaspoon ground turmeric

⅛ teaspoon ground white pepper

1 red bell pepper

Place the eggs in a large saucepan and cover with 1 to 2 inches of water. Set the pot over medium-high heat and bring to a boil. Turn off the heat, cover the pot with a lid, and let sit for 10 to 12 minutes.

Fill a large bowl with ice and cold water to make an ice bath. Set aside.

Transfer the cooked eggs to the ice bath and let cool completely.

In a large sealable container, stir together the water and food coloring until a uniform color. Peel the eggs and add them to the colored water. Cover and refrigerate for 4 hours.

Remove the eggs from the water and cut the eggs in half lengthwise. Using a teaspoon, carefully scoop the yolks into a large bowl and set aside the whites.

To the yolks, add the mayonnaise, gherkins, mustard, Old Bay, turmeric, and white pepper. Stir until the yolks are smooth and the mixture is combined. Transfer to a piping bag and pipe the egg yolk filling into the egg whites, covering the top of the eggs.

Cut the bell pepper into tiny bow ties and place on top of the eggs.

Refrigerate until ready to serve.

Pompompurin Yogurt Parfait

Pompompurin loves anything made with milk, so it just makes sense that his preferred morning meal is a pretty parfait. Pure mango puree gives it a golden shine, topped with tangy Greek yogurt for good measure. A little crunch goes a long way, so pecans and shredded coconut top it off. But it doesn't end there—what's that on top? A sweet chocolate disk, of course, acting as an ode to Pompompurin's own dandy beret.

1 ripe mango (6 ounces), peeled and seeded
¼ cup sweetened oat milk
⅛ teaspoon ground nutmeg
⅛ teaspoon kosher salt
½ cup vanilla Greek yogurt
1 tablespoon chopped pecans
1 tablespoon shredded coconut
1 tablespoon honey
1 chocolate disk

In a blender, combine the mango, oat milk, nutmeg, and salt. Blend until smooth and combined. Pour the mango puree into a parfait glass.

Top the mango with the yogurt.

Sprinkle on the pecans and coconut.

Drizzle the honey over everything.

Place the chocolate disk on top, at a jaunty angle, to serve.

CHAPTER TWO

Lovely Lunches

For Hello Kitty, there are so many fun possibilities at lunchtime. She can visit her friends and enjoy a full day of food and fun. If it's a sunny day, she might visit Keroppi and have a lovely picnic outdoors by Donut Pond. For a day indoors, she might go with Cinnamoroll to eat at the Cinnamon Cafe. If her friends are busy, Hello Kitty can enjoy some quiet time with a solo meal at home with a good book.

If you're on your own and have a lunch break, make the most of it. It means you can eat as you please. Hangyodon Sesame Noodles (page 27) are always a good midday choice. A favorite of Hangydon, noodles are his go-to meal and he's usually eating alone. No shame in that. Solo meals make for some of the best company. When the busy week catches up to you or if you're on the go, something portable is ideal. You might want to grab a My Melody Musubi (page 34) or some Pompompurin Pork Buns (page 28). Both foods can be slipped easily into your bag while you head out to finish off a day of activities.

Meeting up with pals for a potluck? Kiki and Lala know that LittleTwinStars' Crispy Pork Wontons (page 31) always feed a crowd. There's nothing like sharing a plate of crispy star-shaped treats and catching up with your closest friends. A quick one-on-one chat session for a more intimate affair, Tuxedosam would put together an elegant Tuxedosam Bow Tie Pasta Salad (page 36). As cheeky as his attire, this light meal is as delightful to look at as it is delicious.

Lunch is a time to stretch your palate creatively and take advantage of a well-earned midday break. If you're lucky enough to meet up with friends and coworkers, sharing food is a great way to learn about other people and make new friends. Enjoy every bite and relish the fact that you've made it halfway through the day.

Cinnamoroll Ricotta Toast

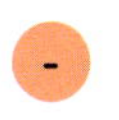

At the Cinnamon Cafe, Cinnamoroll is a customer favorite when he cuddles up in their laps while they order. His sweet face is reflected in the menu with this savory lunch. A garlicky toast smothered with marinara and toppings, this serving for one fulfills a pizza craving thanks to the healthy dollop of ricotta that looks just like Cinnamoroll's floppy ears. It's comfort food and cuddles all around.

1 tablespoon unsalted butter, softened

1 tablespoon parmesan cheese

1 garlic clove, minced

1 slice sourdough bread

2 tablespoons marinara sauce

¼ cup sliced pepperoni

⅓ cup ricotta

2 teaspoons lemon zest

¼ teaspoon onion powder

¼ teaspoon kosher salt

2 black olives

1 small ham slice

In a small bowl, stir together the butter, parmesan, and garlic. Spread the garlic butter onto the sourdough bread. Toast the bread in a toaster oven until golden brown, about 2 minutes.

Line a small baking sheet with parchment paper and place the toast on it.

Spread the marinara on the garlic toast and top with the pepperoni.

In a small bowl, stir together the ricotta, lemon zest, onion powder, and salt. Transfer the mixture to a piping bag. Pipe Cinnamoroll's head and ears onto the toast.

Broil in a toaster oven until bubbling, 1 to 2 minutes.

Place the olives for eyes and the ham for Cinnamoroll's cheeks, to create his face. Serve immediately.

Continues on next page

Hangyodon Sesame Noodles

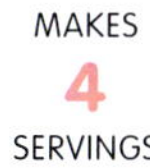

There's nothing more comforting than a big bowl of noodles. As one of Hangyodon's favorite foods, this dish is super flavorful thanks to a fragrant sauce made with pungent vinegars, tangy chili crisp, and creamy peanut butter. To balance all that flavor, the noodles are served with cool, crunchy cucumber and carrot. If you're home alone, like Hangyodon usually is, go ahead and eat them right out of the pan, or serve them cold if you can wait that long!

3 tablespoons smooth peanut butter

2 tablespoons soy sauce

1 tablespoon black vinegar

1 tablespoon rice vinegar

1 tablespoon chili crisp

2 teaspoons packed light brown sugar

1 teaspoon sesame oil

4 garlic cloves, minced

2 tablespoons olive oil

15 ounces yakisoba stir-fry noodles

2 tablespoons water

1 medium carrot, julienned

1 medium cucumber, julienned

2 green onions, diced

2 teaspoons toasted sesame seeds

In a small saucepan over medium heat, combine the peanut butter, soy sauce, black vinegar, rice vinegar, chili crisp, brown sugar, sesame oil, and garlic. Cook until bubbly, 1 to 2 minutes. Remove from the heat.

In a large skillet over medium heat, heat the olive oil. Add the noodles and water. Cook until the noodles are loose and warmed through, 1 to 2 minutes. Add the peanut butter sauce to the skillet and toss the noodles in the sauce to coat well. Transfer to a serving bowl.

Top the noodles with the carrot, cucumber, and green onions. Sprinkle with the sesame seeds.

Serve immediately or refrigerate to serve cold.

Pompompurin Pork Buns

MAKES **12** BUNS

Pompompurin loves to eat. Bouncy and soft foods are his weakness and these soft buns are always a treat. Homemade dough fluffs up as it bakes in the oven, and when broken open, reveals a succulent filling of flavorful pork—a classic combination. But you won't be able to stop at just one; picture-perfect pork buns are irresistible little treasures and a pocketful of pork puts a spring in Pompompurin's step.

FOR THE PORK

1 pound diced pork belly

2 tablespoons soy sauce

3 tablespoons honey

3 tablespoons oyster sauce

1 teaspoon rice vinegar

3 garlic cloves, minced

½ teaspoon minced fresh ginger

1 teaspoon Chinese five-spice powder

¼ teaspoon black pepper

FOR THE BUNS

3¾ cups bread flour, plus more for dusting

½ cup water

1 envelope (2¼ teaspoons) active dry yeast

¾ cup whole milk, heated to 110°F

¼ cup granulated sugar

½ teaspoon kosher salt

2 tablespoons unsalted butter, melted

1 large egg, lightly beaten

2 tablespoons olive oil, for greasing

FOR THE EGG WASH

1 large egg

1 tablespoon water

FOR THE SIMPLE SYRUP

2 tablespoons granulated sugar

2 tablespoons boiling water

Edible ink pen, for decorating

To make the pork: In a skillet over medium-high heat, add the pork, soy sauce, honey, oyster sauce, rice vinegar, garlic, ginger, five-spice powder, and pepper. Cook for 4 to 5 minutes, until cooked through. Let cool, slightly. Refrigerate until ready to use.

To make the buns: In a medium saucepan over medium heat, whisk ½ cup of the bread flour with the water to make a roux. Cook until thickened, 2 to 3 minutes. Remove from the heat and transfer to a bowl. Set aside to cool.

In the bowl of a stand mixer fitted with a dough hook attachment, sprinkle the yeast over the warm milk and let sit for 10 minutes, until foamy.

Stir in the sugar, salt, butter, egg, and roux. Slowly add the remaining flour, until combined. Knead for 8 to 10 minutes until smooth.

Grease a large bowl with oil and transfer the dough to it. Cover with plastic wrap and let rise for 1 hour, until doubled in size.

Line a baking sheet with parchment paper.

Punch down the dough and turn it out onto a lightly floured surface. Knead it slightly by hand, two to three times, until smooth. Divide the dough into twelve equal pieces and roll into balls. Take one ball and flatten into a circle. Place 2 tablespoons of pork filling into the center, pulling up the edges and pinching it close. Place the filled bun on the prepared baking sheet. Repeat with the remaining dough and filling. Cover the buns with a clean kitchen towel and let rise for 1 hour.

Preheat the oven to 350°F.

To make the egg wash: In a small bowl, whisk the egg and water to blend. Use a pastry brush to brush the buns with egg wash.

Bake until golden brown, 20 minutes.

To make the simple syrup: In a small bowl, stir together the sugar and water. Immediately brush onto the hot buns. Let cool on a wire rack.

Use the edible ink pen to add Pompompurin's face details, then serve.

Kuromi Pickled Radish Salad

MAKES 4 SERVINGS

Some people can't resist foods like cakes or fruit, but not Kuromi; she's distinctly herself and loves shallots! Her flavor profile leans fragrant and savory, and this salad takes those sharp flavors and elevates them. Not only that, a beautiful mix of Kuromi's classic black and pink colors are reflected with the perfect blend of radishes and black sesame seeds—a unique taste for a unique personality.

1 English cucumber, peeled and thinly sliced

1 bunch radishes, rinsed, dried, and thinly sliced

1 medium shallot, sliced

2 garlic cloves, peeled and smashed

2 tablespoons torn fresh fennel fronds

½ cup champagne vinegar

1 teaspoon kosher salt

¼ teaspoon ground black pepper

1 teaspoon black sesame seeds

In a sealable container, combine the cucumber, radishes, shallot, garlic, and fennel fronds. Add the vinegar, salt, and pepper and stir gently to combine. Cover and refrigerate for 3 hours.

Sprinkle the black sesame seeds on top to serve.

LittleTwinStars' Crispy Pork Wontons

MAKES **48** WONTONS

Lala's star wand magically makes snacks appear, but she hardly needs it as she's a whiz in the kitchen. When it comes to lunchtime, the stars align again with these crispy, delicious fried wontons. Pointy just like the twin siblings' favorite shape, these little pockets are filled with a tangy blend of pork and seasonings. They're easy to make on your own, but they're even better when you have someone to give you a hand in the kitchen. Luckily, Lala has her brother, Kiki, to help.

1 pound ground pork

1 (8-ounce) can water chestnuts, drained and minced

2 garlic cloves, minced

2 green onions, diced

1 teaspoon minced fresh ginger

3 tablespoons oyster sauce

2 tablespoons soy sauce

2 teaspoons rice vinegar

½ teaspoon ground black pepper

48 wonton wrappers

4 cups vegetable oil

1 cup sweet chili sauce

Line a plate with parchment paper.

In a large bowl, stir together the ground pork, water chestnuts, garlic, green onions, ginger, oyster sauce, soy sauce, vinegar, and pepper until just combined.

Working with one wrapper at a time, place a teaspoonful of filling into the center of a wonton wrapper. Use your finger to rub water on all four edges of the wrapper, then bring together two opposite corners to form a point, pinching just the tips to seal. Bring up the remaining two corners to meet, pinching all the edges to seal, to form a four-pointed star. Place the star on the prepared plate and cover with a clean kitchen towel. Repeat with the remaining filling and wrappers.

In a Dutch oven over medium heat, heat the oil to 350°F. Working in batches, carefully place the wontons in the hot oil and deep-fry until golden brown, 3 to 4 minutes. Transfer to a wire rack to drain.

Serve with the sweet chili sauce for dipping.

Continues on next page

Crispy pork wontons have to be the happiest food ever. They're little pouches of surprise filling, like tiny star-shaped presents. The fun part is you can fold them in a variety of ways, no magic star wand necessary. They all begin the same, with a flat square wrapper. Start with an easy shape, a half fold. Just fold one side to the other to make a rectangle, sealing up the edges. For the next shape, try a pyramid: take the four corners of the wrapper and bring them to a point, pinching the edges closed. Finally, try making a little pleated purse. First, fold the wrapper into a triangle shape, then pleat the top to form ruffles. Make sure you seal it tightly so the filling doesn't fall out. Follow Lala's lead of getting Kiki to help her in the kitchen, and find a friend to help you try these different dumpling folds.

Pochacco Fruit Sando

Pochacco enjoys banana ice cream, carrots, and anything vegetarian, but that doesn't mean food options for lunch have to be boring. In fact, vegetarian lunches are some of the most exciting. A light lunch of fruit can be turned into a beautiful creamy sandwich that's lighter than air. Filled to the brim with homemade whipped cream, fresh berries are nestled in between like a fanciful fluffy bite of comfort. A dainty yet elegant meal any day of the week.

½ cup heavy cream

1 tablespoon powdered sugar

¼ teaspoon clear vanilla extract

⅛ teaspoon kosher salt

2 slices white bread

5 fresh strawberries, hulled

In a medium bowl, combine the heavy cream, powdered sugar, vanilla, and salt. Use a hand-held mixer to whip the mixture until stiff peaks form and hold.

Spread half of the whipped cream mixture on one slice of bread.

Arrange the strawberries in a diagonal line.

Cover the strawberries completely with the remaining whipped cream. Top with the second slice of bread.

Wrap the sandwich tightly with plastic wrap to compress it. Refrigerate for 25 minutes.

Remove the plastic wrap. Cut off the crusts, then slice diagonally down the middle of the sandwich across the strawberries to serve.

My Melody Musubi

The forest of Mariland, where My Melody was born, is a perfect place for a picnic. Invite a few friends and make it a potluck. Have them bring snacks and drinks, while you provide the most portable of foods—musubi. Rice and luncheon meat is already the perfect pairing, but when it's shaped like My Melody, it becomes the cutest snack on the go to share with friends.

4 cups short-grain white rice

6 cups water

1 (12-ounce) can luncheon meat (such as Spam)

1 large egg

1 tablespoon vegetable oil

1 nori sheet

Rinse the rice in a fine-mesh sieve four to five times, until the water runs clear.

In a large pot over high heat, combine the rice and water. Bring to a boil. Cover the pan and reduce the heat to maintain a simmer. Cook until the water is absorbed, 20 minutes. Remove from the heat and let sit, covered, for 10 minutes.

Cut the luncheon meat into nine slices.

In a large skillet over medium heat, cook the luncheon meat until heated through, 2 to 3 minutes on each side. Let cool slightly.

In a small bowl, whisk the egg. Set aside.

In a small skillet over medium heat, heat the oil. Add the egg and cook until just set, 1 to 2 minutes. Remove from the pan and let cool slightly.

Carefully shape the hot rice into nine 2 by 4-inch rectangles.

Cut the cooked luncheon meat into My Melody shapes and place them on the rice rectangles.

Cut small bows out of the egg and place on the left side of her hood.

Cut out face details from the nori sheet to complete the face.

Serve immediately.

Tuxedosam Bow Tie Pasta Salad

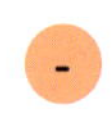

MAKES **10** SERVINGS

Tuxedosam loves to eat, but his true passion is his bow tie collection. Style is important to him, so it's no wonder he finds inspiration everywhere he looks, even in his meals. These bow ties are dapper but don't wear them—they're made of pasta. Tossed with a variety of savory accoutrements, this pasta salad is as colorful as Tuxedosam's personality, with unexpected flavors in every bite.

FOR THE DRESSING

½ cup extra-virgin olive oil

⅓ cup red wine vinegar

1 tablespoon fresh lemon juice

1 tablespoon chopped fresh parsley

1 teaspoon Dijon mustard

1 teaspoon dried oregano

½ teaspoon kosher salt

¼ teaspoon ground black pepper

2 garlic cloves, minced

FOR THE SALAD

1 (16-ounce) box bow tie pasta

1½ cups halved cherry tomatoes

½ cup sliced black olives, drained

½ cup corn

½ cup diced green bell pepper

½ cup diced red onion

½ cup chopped salami

½ cup mini mozzarella balls

To make the dressing: In a small bowl, whisk the olive oil, vinegar, lemon juice, parsley, mustard, oregano, salt, pepper, and garlic to combine. Set aside.

To make the pasta: Bring a large pot of water to a boil over high heat. Carefully add the pasta and cook according to the package directions. Drain, but do not rinse. Let cool for 10 minutes.

To make the salad: In a large bowl, toss together the pasta, tomatoes, olives, corn, bell pepper, onion, salami, and mozzarella.

Pour the dressing over the salad and toss again to coat.

Refrigerate until ready to serve.

Chococat Roast Chicken

MAKES **8** SERVINGS

Chococat loves good food and hanging out with his friends. With this roast chicken he can do both, because it is big enough to share with others. Flavored with just the right amount of seasoning, the fragrant herbs and crispy skin make this chicken the perfect lunch to impress your friends. If you happen to have leftovers, use them to make other dishes or pack up a take-home care package for your guests.

- **1 (3-pound) whole chicken**
- **½ cup (1 stick) unsalted butter, at room temperature**
- **1 tablespoon kosher salt**
- **2 teaspoons onion powder**
- **1 teaspoon ground black pepper**
- **1 sweet onion, quartered**
- **6 garlic cloves, peeled**
- **1 rosemary sprig**
- **1 thyme sprig**

Preheat the oven to 425°F.

Remove and discard the neck and giblets from the chicken.

Rub the butter on the outside of the chicken, under the skin, and inside the cavity.

Sprinkle the chicken with salt, onion powder, and pepper.

Place the onion, garlic, rosemary, and thyme inside the cavity.

Tie the legs together with kitchen twine and tuck the wings under the body. Place the chicken on a rack in a roasting pan.

Roast, basting the chicken every 30 minutes with the juices in the pan, until golden brown and an instant-read thermometer reads 165°F, 1½ hours. Tent with aluminum foil and let rest for 15 minutes.

Slice to serve.

Gorgeoustown Ramen

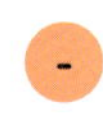

MAKES
1
SERVING

Badtz-maru loves living in Gorgeoustown because there is so much good food on every corner. You'll never have a bad meal there. It's easy to replicate those memorable restaurant dishes at home, even if you're not a top chef. This recipe is an easy way to use store-bought ramen and turn it into something special. It's all about the add-ons. Top it off with Badtz-maru's favorite crunchy ramen snack, and you'll get a crispy bite with every scoop.

FOR THE RAMEN

2 cups chicken broth

1 tablespoon white miso paste

1 (3-ounce) package instant ramen noodles

1 large egg

1 teaspoon soy sauce

½ teaspoon chili oil

FOR THE TOPPINGS

¼ cup baby spinach

1 tablespoon crunchy ramen snack

1 green onion, diced

½ teaspoon toasted sesame seeds

To make the ramen: In a large saucepan over medium-high heat, combine the chicken broth and miso paste. Bring to a boil. Add the instant noodles and boil for 2 minutes.

In a small bowl, crack the egg and lightly beat it with a fork. Swirl the noodles and slowly pour in the egg. Add the soy sauce. Cook until the egg has just set, 1 minute. Transfer to a bowl and drizzle with the chili oil.

To finish: Top the ramen with the baby spinach, crunchy ramen, green onion, and sesame seeds. Serve immediately.

The best thing about ramen at home is making it uniquely yours. Your taste is the barometer and you can add just about anything. If you've got high standards, like Badtz-maru, add some quality ingredients like a rich beef broth or truffle oil. Top off the bowl with a lovely piece of fresh salmon and some furikake. Or maybe go simple and add some green onions and carrots from your own backyard. Whatever you choose to add to your noodles, stretch your imagination and play with flavors to create an exceptional dish you can call your own.

Teruteru Rice Balls

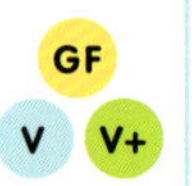

A friend of Keroppi, Teruteru is a sunshine doll who can predict the weather, which is a great talent to have, especially when you're planning a picnic around Donut Pond. A sunny day is the best day because you can make it a fun day with friends. Keroppi's favorite things to eat are rice balls, and this version is dressed up to look just like his sunny friend. Filled with a healthy helping of veggies, they're perfect for a pleasant park day out with friends.

2 cups short-grain white rice

3 cups water

½ teaspoon kosher salt

½ cup mixed vegetables, cooked

2 teaspoons furikake

Nori, for decoration

Rinse the rice in a fine-mesh sieve four to five times, until the water runs clear.

In a large saucepan over high heat, combine the rice and water. Bring to a boil. Cover the pan and reduce the heat to maintain a simmer. Cook until the water is absorbed, 20 minutes. Remove from the heat and let sit, covered, for 10 minutes.

Fluff the rice with a fork and sprinkle with the salt. Let cool slightly. Divide the rice into eight equal portions and place each on its own plastic wrap.

Place 1 tablespoon of the vegetables into the center of each rice portion. Sprinkle each with ¼ teaspoon of furikake.

Use plastic wrap to mold the rice into a round shape enclosing the vegetables.

Add nori to create a Teruteru face.

Teruteru is named after teru teru bōzu, Japanese sunshine dolls hung outside to summon sunny weather. These little rice balls hail happiness all on their own, and you can make each unique with different ingredients. Try filling them with scrambled egg to really bring about the sunshine or some pickled radish for a nice sour kick. You can even fill them with protein, like shredded Chococat Roast Chicken (page 37). Just make sure to take some when you visit Chococat. Sharing these little Teruteru rice balls with friends is the best part of making them.

Hello Kitty Tomato Soup with Grilled Cheese Croutons

Hello Kitty's iconic red bow is the inspiration for everything, including this fun lunchtime meal. Red like the bow itself, this tomato soup is warm and nourishing, made with healthy vegetables and savory seasonings. A filling meal on its own, the distinguished bow appears again, as a shaped grilled cheese to top it all off. Share this happy bow-themed meal with friends to make the day even sweeter.

FOR THE SOUP

2 tablespoons olive oil

1 medium sweet onion, diced

2 medium carrots, diced

1 medium shallot, diced

1 tablespoon tomato paste

1 tablespoon cornstarch

4 cups vegetable stock

1 (28-ounce) can diced roasted tomatoes

1 teaspoon dried basil

1 teaspoon dried oregano

1 teaspoon dried thyme

1½ teaspoons kosher salt

½ teaspoon ground black pepper

½ cup coconut milk

FOR THE GRILLED CHEESE

½ cup (1 stick) unsalted butter, at room temperature

2 garlic cloves, minced

2 tablespoon grated parmesan cheese

8 slices white bread

8 slices sharp cheddar cheese

To make the soup: In a Dutch oven over medium heat, heat the olive oil. Add the sweet onion, carrots, and shallot. Cook until softened, 5 minutes. Stir in the tomato paste. Sprinkle over the cornstarch. Cook, stirring, until thickened, 1 minute more.

Pour in the vegetable stock and tomatoes. Stir in the basil, oregano, thyme, salt, and pepper. Bring the soup to a boil, then reduce the heat to low. Cover the pot and simmer until the vegetables have softened, 30 minutes.

Turn off the heat and stir in the coconut milk. Use an immersion blender and puree the soup until smooth.

To make the grilled cheese: In a small bowl, stir together the butter, garlic, and parmesan. Spread 1 tablespoon of the butter mixture onto one side of each slice of bread.

Place four slices of bread, buttered-side down, into a skillet over medium-high heat. Top each slice with two cheddar slices, then top with the remaining four slices of bread, buttered-side up. Cook until browned and the cheese has melted, 2 minutes on each side. Cut each sandwich into two bow tie shapes, creating 8 total.

Ladle the soup into bowls and serve with the bow tie–shaped grilled cheese.

CHAPTER THREE

Delightful Dinners

For Hello Kitty and her friends, the end of the day is for winding down and reflecting, and an excellent meal is a big part of that. Food in the evening hits differently. The meals are more filling, the flavors a little richer, and, all in all, dinner gives you the satisfaction of a job well done after a long day.

A big bowl of stew is always a good option to sink into after a long day. With more time to develop deep flavors, Chococat knows the warmth of a succulent chocolate stew (see page 50) can't be beat, thanks to its unique ingredient. Who knew chocolate could add such a complex flavor to a savory dish? In the same way, Hangyodon finds comfort in the richness of a seafood pasta (see page 56). The pasta is light yet filling, and with an abundance of shrimp and scallops, it's a true tribute to the sea.

Kuromi loves all things October, which is why Kuromi's Stuffed Kabocha Squash (page 64) is the ideal meal for her. Dark on the outside but bright and interesting on the inside, this dish takes time to make but is worth the wait. All these dishes can feel like a warm hug, helping you forget your troubles at the end of a long day.

Hearty meals are rich and filling, and sometimes a lighter meal is in order so you can save room for dessert. Sushi (see page 48) is always a good option, especially for Badtz-maru; maybe just don't indulge as much as he would. He doesn't know when to stop! Another lovely light meal is My Melody Somen Salad (page 58). There's nothing like a satisfying slurp, and afterward you'll have plenty of room for a sweet treat.

Whatever you choose, think of dinner as a delicious reward for making it through the day. Enjoy all it has to offer, savor every flavor, and take time to taste every ingredient. Hello Kitty and her friends work as hard as they play, and an abundant end-of-day meal is the best way to celebrate your accomplishments.

Keroppi Miso Salmon

MAKES **2** SERVINGS

Keroppi and his friends always find a lot to do around Donut Pond. It's a great gathering place to hang out and do a little fishing. Having a chef in the house means Keroppi can take his catches home and have his mother cook up a delicious meal in no time. This flavorful salmon is marinated in miso, and broiling the fish right at the end is what makes this dish so mouthwateringly delicious.

2 tablespoons white miso

2 tablespoons mirin

1 tablespoon tamari

1 tablespoon granulated sugar

1 garlic clove, minced

2 (6-ounce) salmon fillets

Cooked rice, for serving

In a sealable container, stir together the miso, mirin, tamari, sugar, and garlic.

Add the salmon to the marinade and turn to coat. Cover and refrigerate for 2 hours.

Preheat the oven's broiler. Line a baking sheet with nonstick aluminum foil.

Remove the salmon from the marinade and place it, skin-side down, on the prepared baking sheet. Discard the excess marinade.

Broil until crispy and an instant-read thermometer reads 140°F, 10 minutes.

Serve with rice.

Badtz-maru Sushi

MAKES
3
SERVINGS

One of Badtz-maru's favorite foods is sushi, and he certainly gets his fill in Gorgeoustown. Sushi doesn't always have to be expensive or over the top; sometimes it's nice to keep it simple. Making a simple sushi dinner at home is easy. Layered veggies and imitation crab make this an effortless dish that will keep you coming back for more. An easy meal will keep you feeling full and happy. Even Badtz-maru can't argue with that.

¼ cup rice vinegar

3 tablespoons granulated sugar

½ teaspoon kosher salt

2 cups short-grain white rice

3 cups water

2 nori sheets

1 medium cucumber, peeled and sliced into spears

1 medium carrot, julienned

1 avocado, peeled, halved, pitted, and sliced

8 ounces imitation crabmeat, shredded

¼ cup Japanese mayonnaise

In a small saucepan over medium heat, combine the vinegar, sugar, and salt. Bring to a low simmer and cook until the sugar dissolves, 1 minute. Remove from the heat.

Rinse the rice in a fine-mesh sieve four to five times, until the water runs clear.

In a large saucepan over high heat, combine the rice and water. Bring to a boil. Cover the pan and reduce the heat to maintain a simmer. Cook until the water is absorbed, 20 minutes. Remove from the heat and let sit, covered, for 10 minutes.

Fluff the rice with a fork and sprinkle it with the vinegar mixture. Let cool for 10 minutes.

Cover a bamboo rolling mat with plastic wrap. Place a nori sheet, shiny-side down, on the plastic wrap. Spread half the rice over the nori sheet, leaving a ¼ inch border at the bottom edge.

Place half of the cucumber, half of the carrot, and half of the avocado onto the center of the nori sheet.

In a small bowl, stir together the imitation crab and mayonnaise. Spoon half the crab mixture over the vegetables.

Pick up the bottom edge of the mat, folding the bottom edge of the sheet up, and roll the sushi tightly while pressing. Repeat with the remaining ingredients.

Use a knife to cut each roll into 1-inch pieces to serve.

Chococat Chocolate Stew

Chocolate is mostly known as a sweet treat, but its unique essence can lend itself nicely to savory dishes as well. Chococat will take chocolate any way he can get it, and this nice surprise adds depth of flavor and richness to dinner dishes like this delicious beef stew. Invite friends over and see if they can identify the secret ingredient; they might be surprised!

FOR THE BEEF

2 pounds beef chuck, cubed

3 tablespoons cornstarch

1 teaspoon kosher salt

1 teaspoon ground black pepper

FOR THE STEW

2 tablespoons olive oil

2 tablespoons unsalted butter

1 medium onion, diced

2 celery stalks, diced

2 garlic cloves, minced

4 cups beef broth

1 cup red wine

2 thyme sprigs

1 bay leaf

1 pound small creamer potatoes, halved

2 carrots, cut into 1-inch pieces

1½ ounces dark chocolate

½ teaspoon kosher salt

½ teaspoon ground black pepper

Chopped fresh parsley, for garnish

To make the beef: In a large dish, toss the beef in the cornstarch, salt, and pepper.

To make the stew: In a large Dutch oven over medium-high heat, heat the olive oil. Add the beef and cook, turning, to brown, 5 minutes. Transfer the beef to a bowl.

Add the butter to melt, then add the onion, celery, and garlic and sauté until softened, 5 minutes.

Return the beef to the pot and pour in the beef broth and wine. Bring to a boil.

Add the thyme and bay leaf. Lower the heat to maintain a simmer and cover the pot. Cook for 2 hours.

Add the potatoes and carrots, re-cover the pot, and continue simmering until the beef is tender, 30 minutes. Discard the thyme and bay leaf.

Stir in the dark chocolate until melted.

Season with salt and pepper.

Garnish with parsley to serve.

The best thing about big one-pot meals like chocolate stew is the leftovers. If you have just enough for a small bowl, it can pair nicely as a side dish to create a whole new meal. Teruteru Rice Balls (page 40) or Pompompurin Potato Croquettes (page 52) are lovely options to pair with a bowl. Pompompurin would agree that the crunchy outside of the croquettes is good for dipping into the rich stew. If you'd rather have something lighter, Tuxedosam would argue that his Bow Tie Pasta Salad (page 36) would be the ideal pairing. A light pasta served alongside the full-bodied stew makes a lovely balanced meal.

Pompompurin Potato Croquettes

Pompompurin has a very busy daily schedule—mostly filled with doing his pudding exercises and taking naps. Pretty intense. To take a break from all that activity, he needs a good snack. Crispy and full of veggies, these crunchy croquettes are a delight. Great all on their own, they also pair well with Pochacco Veggie Curry (page 61). Think of these fried treats as a reward for a full day of living your best life.

2 large russet potatoes, peeled and diced
½ cup corn
½ cup peas
½ teaspoon garlic powder
½ teaspoon onion powder
½ teaspoon kosher salt
¼ teaspoon ground black pepper
¾ cup all-purpose flour
½ teaspoon seasoned salt
2 large eggs
1 teaspoon mirin
2 cups panko bread crumbs
4 cups vegetable oil
Tonkatsu sauce, for garnish

In a large pot, combine the potatoes with enough water to cover by 1 inch. Bring to a boil over medium-high heat, then reduce the heat to low and simmer until fork-tender, about 15 minutes. Drain, transfer to a large bowl, and mash the potatoes.

Fold in the corn, peas, garlic powder, onion powder, kosher salt, and pepper. Form the mixture into six patties.

Create a frying station with three shallow dishes. In the first dish, whisk the flour and seasoned salt to combine. In the second, beat the eggs with the mirin. Pour the panko into the third dish.

Dredge the patties in flour, shaking off the excess, then dip into the beaten egg, and, finally, coat in the panko.

In a large Dutch oven over medium-high heat, heat the oil to 350°F.

Carefully add the patties to the hot oil and fry until golden brown, 2 to 3 minutes on each side. Transfer to a wire rack to drain.

Pipe tonkatsu sauce to create Pompompurin's face details and hat, then serve.

Pompompurin's dream of getting bigger and bigger means he has a lot of ingredients on hand. These potato croquettes can be doctored up with anything you might have in the fridge. Try adding a cube of mozzarella into the filling for a gracefully grand cheese pull when you bite into it. Leftover luncheon meat from making My Melody Musubi (page 34) is a nice touch for a salty addition to the stuffing. If you invite Badtz-maru over, he might prank you and fill the croquette with something like candy. Make sure you keep an eye on him when he's in the kitchen!

Tuxedosam Shrimp Coquilles

MAKES
8
SERVINGS

The always fashionable Tuxedosam knows how to dress up for a good meal, especially if it's seafood. His favorite dish is shrimp coquilles, and it's as elegant as his bow tie. Shrimp in a creamy white sauce, topped with a crunchy bread crumb mixture, and all served up in a fancy seashell. It's a meal fit for a king—or, in this case, a penguin.

FOR THE SAUCE

2 tablespoons unsalted butter

¼ cup all-purpose flour

1 teaspoon Dijon mustard

1½ cups whole milk

½ teaspoon kosher salt

¼ teaspoon ground nutmeg

¼ teaspoon ground white pepper

FOR THE SHRIMP

1 pound raw medium shrimp, peeled and deveined

2 tablespoons unsalted butter

1 medium shallot, minced

1 tablespoon fresh lemon juice

8 ovenproof seafood shells

1 tablespoon olive oil

FOR THE TOPPING

½ cup bread crumbs

¼ cup panko bread crumbs

¼ cup shredded Swiss cheese

2 tablespoons unsalted butter, melted

½ teaspoon kosher salt

¼ teaspoon ground black pepper

2 teaspoons fresh parsley, chopped

To make the sauce: In a small saucepan over medium heat, melt the butter. Whisk in the flour and mustard and cook until lightly browned, 4 minutes. Whisk in the milk, salt, nutmeg, and white pepper. Adjust the heat to medium-low and simmer until thickened, 6 to 8 minutes. Remove from the heat.

To make the shrimp: In a skillet over medium heat, add the butter and the shallot. Cook until softened, 1 minute. Add the shrimp and cook until pink, 2 to 3 minutes. Pour over the lemon juice. Remove from heat and stir in the sauce.

Preheat the oven to 400°F. Line a baking sheet with slightly crumpled aluminum foil to hold the shells steady. Grease the shells with olive oil.

Spoon the shrimp mixture into the prepared shells, dividing it evenly.

To make the topping: In a small bowl, stir together the bread crumbs, panko, Swiss cheese, melted butter, salt, and black pepper. Add a scoop of topping onto the filled shells.

Bake until browned, 10 minutes.

Garnish with parsley to serve.

Hangyodon Seafood Pasta

MAKES **8** SERVINGS

Hangyodon doesn't express a lot of emotion, but in his heart he's a lonely romantic. All he wants is to spend time with someone, maybe over a nice bowl of ambrosial pasta. He'll never skip an ocean ingredient-filled meal. Savory shrimp and sweet scallops take this pasta dish above and beyond, each bite better than the next. Hangyodon just needs a friend to share it with.

1 (16-ounce) package angel hair pasta

1 pound scallops

2 tablespoons olive oil

Kosher salt and ground black pepper

2 tablespoons unsalted butter

1 large shallot, sliced

4 garlic cloves, minced

1 pound raw large shrimp, peeled and deveined

1 teaspoon fresh oregano, minced

1 cup white wine

2 tablespoons fresh lemon juice

1½ cups cherry tomatoes, halved

½ cup pitted green olives, drained

1 cup baby spinach

⅓ cup grated parmesan cheese

1 tablespoon chopped fresh parsley

Bring a large pot of water to a boil over high heat. Add the pasta and cook according to the package directions. Reserve ½ cup of the pasta water, then drain the pasta, but do not rinse it.

Pat the scallops dry with a paper towel.

In a large skillet over medium-high heat, heat the olive oil. Add the scallops, being careful not to overcrowd the skillet. Cook for 2 to 3 minutes. Season with ½ teaspoon salt and ¼ teaspoon pepper. Flip the scallops and cook until golden brown, firm, and opaque, 2 to 3 minutes. Transfer to a plate and cover with aluminum foil to keep warm.

In the same skillet over medium-high heat, melt the butter. Add the shallot and garlic and cook until fragrant, 2 minutes.

Add the shrimp. Cook until pink, 2 to 3 minutes on each side. Sprinkle with the oregano.

Pour in the wine and cook until slightly reduced, 2 minutes, then stir in the lemon juice.

Add the drained pasta, tomatoes, olives, spinach, parmesan, ½ teaspoon salt, and ¼ teaspoon pepper. Toss with the reserved pasta water to thicken.

Top with the scallops and parsley to serve.

My Melody Somen Salad

MAKES **4** SERVINGS

The color pink brings so much joy; it's the color of My Melody's favorite hood, and it's even the color of noodles! These somen noodles are white and sakura pink, the exact colors inspired by My Melody. Light and easy to make, this refreshing salad is a great summer meal on hot days—as tasty as it is cute.

FOR THE DRESSING

1½ tablespoons champagne vinegar

1 tablespoon vegetable oil

1 tablespoon sesame oil

1 tablespoon granulated sugar

1 tablespoon soy sauce

¼ teaspoon kosher salt

FOR THE SALAD

6 ounces (2 bundles) pink somen noodles

3 ounces (1 bundle) white somen noodles

1 tablespoon olive oil

1 large egg, lightly beaten

4 ounces iceberg lettuce, shredded

1 teaspoon sesame seeds

1 green onion, chopped

1 nori sheet

To make the dressing: In a sealable jar, combine the vinegar, vegetable oil, sesame oil, sugar, soy sauce, and salt. Cover and shake to combine. Set aside.

To make the salad: Bring a large pot of water to a boil over high heat. Add the pink somen noodles. Cook for 2 minutes. Drain, rinse in cold water, and set aside.

Refill the pot with water and bring it to a boil over high heat. Add the white somen noodles. Cook for 2 minutes. Drain, rinse in cold water, and set aside in a separate bowl.

Place a medium skillet over low heat, pour in the olive oil, use a paper towel to spread it around, then wipe out the excess. Pour in the beaten egg and cook until just set, 1 minute. When the edges are dry and the middle is just cooked, transfer to a cutting board. Cut out a 1-inch flower and a ½-inch oval from the egg to create My Melody's nose. Set aside. Cut the remaining egg into thin strips.

On a serving platter, arrange the lettuce flat. Add the egg strips, sesame seeds, and green onion.

Arrange the white noodles to create My Melody's face and place the pink noodles above to create her bonnet.

Use the nori to create her eyes and mouth.

Place the reserved yellow egg flower on the right side of her head, and the yellow oval nose onto the face.

Serve with the dressing on the side.

Hello Kitty Pizza

If there's one food that can bring a smile to anyone's face, it's pizza. A cheesy topping is a must, and this one has not one, not two, but four cheeses! You can never have too much cheese. For a kawaii touch, add little bow-shaped bell peppers. Adorable and tasty, this pizza will have you smiling with its sweet, subtle nod to Hello Kitty.

1 red bell pepper

1 tablespoon all-purpose flour, for dusting

16 ounces store-bought pizza dough

2 tablespoons extra-virgin olive oil

2 garlic cloves, minced

1 cup marinara

1 cup shredded mozzarella cheese

½ cup shredded Gruyère cheese

½ cup crumbled feta cheese

¼ cup grated parmesan cheese

6 fresh basil leaves

Cut the bell pepper into small Hello Kitty bow shapes. Set aside.

Preheat the oven to 425°F. Line a baking sheet with parchment paper.

On a lightly floured surface, press and roll the dough into a 12-inch round and place it on the prepared baking sheet.

In a small bowl, stir together the olive oil and garlic. Brush the oil onto the dough.

Spread the marinara evenly over the dough. Sprinkle on the mozzarella, Gruyère, feta, and parmesan. Arrange the bell pepper bows on the pizza.

Bake until the crust is browned, 15 minutes.

Top with torn basil leaves to serve.

Pochacco Veggie Curry

After a long day of playing sports, Pochacco is looking for something flavorful and satisfying. You might think his options are limited, but vegetable dishes don't have to be boring, and this warm curry proves it. Chock-full of healthy veggies like broccoli, carrots, and cauliflower, this hearty dish is a satisfying dinner option. Try serving with Pompompurin Potato Croquettes (page 52) for even more veggie deliciousness!

FOR THE CURRY ROUX

4 tablespoons unsalted butter

½ cup cornstarch

1 tablespoon Japanese curry powder

2 teaspoons ground cumin

½ teaspoon ground allspice

¼ teaspoon ground cloves

FOR THE CURRY

2 tablespoons olive oil

1 large onion, cut into wedges

1 tablespoon peeled, minced fresh ginger

2 garlic cloves, minced

4 carrots, cut on the bias

4 cups vegetable broth

1½ cups broccoli florets

1½ cups cauliflower florets

2 medium russet potatoes, cubed

1 small Asian pear, peeled, cored, and grated

1 tablespoon honey

1 teaspoon kosher salt

1 tablespoon tamari

To make the curry roux: In a small saucepan over medium-low heat, melt the butter.

Turn the heat to low and add the cornstarch. Cook, whisking constantly, until golden brown, 10 minutes. Stir in curry powder, cumin, allspice, and cloves. Transfer to a bowl and set aside to cool.

To make the curry: In a large Dutch oven over medium-high heat, heat the olive oil. Add the onion and sauté until soft, 5 minutes. Stir in the ginger and garlic. Cook until fragrant, 1 minute.

Continues on next page

Stir in the carrots and vegetable broth and bring to a boil.

Stir in the broccoli, cauliflower, potatoes, pear, honey, and salt. Turn the heat to medium-low, cover the pot, and simmer until the vegetables are tender, 25 minutes.

Stir the tamari and roux into the pot. Simmer until thickened, 10 minutes.

LittleTwinStars' Chicken and Biscuits

MAKES **8** SERVINGS

LittleTwinStars Kiki and Lala love being together in the kitchen. Even though Lala is the better cook, Kiki has a lot to contribute, and he likes to help where he can. The signature star on his back is the inspiration for the fluffy biscuits topping this creamy chicken casserole. Their distinct shape makes the dish even more special. With more than enough to share, invite friends over to indulge in this warm, comforting, star-inspired meal.

2 tablespoons unsalted butter

2 carrots, diced

2 celery stalks, diced

8 ounces white mushrooms, quartered

1 small onion, diced

¼ cup cornstarch

1 teaspoon garlic powder

1 teaspoon onion powder

1 teaspoon dried rosemary

1 teaspoon dried thyme

½ teaspoon dried sage

½ teaspoon kosher salt

¼ teaspoon ground black pepper

2 cups chicken broth

1 cup heavy cream

½ cup frozen peas

½ cup frozen corn

3 cups cubed, cooked chicken

1 (8-count) can premade biscuit dough, cut into star shapes

Preheat the oven to 375°F. Grease a 9 by 13-inch baking dish with nonstick cooking spray.

In a Dutch oven over medium-high heat, melt the butter. Add the carrots, celery, mushrooms, and onion and cook until soft, 8 to 10 minutes.

Reduce the heat to low, stir in the cornstarch, and cook for 2 to 3 minutes.

Stir in the garlic powder, onion powder, rosemary, thyme, dried sage, salt, and pepper.

Pour in the chicken broth and cream. Bring to a boil, then turn off the heat.

Stir in the peas, corn, and chicken. Pour the mixture into the prepared dish.

Arrange the star-shaped biscuits on top of the chicken mixture.

Bake until the biscuits have browned, 25 minutes. Let cool slightly before serving.

Kuromi's Stuffed Kabocha Squash

MAKES 6 SERVINGS

Kuromi's love of October inspired this Japanese favorite. A close member of the pumpkin family, kabocha is dark green on the outside, making it seem a bit menacing—but the soft orange interior is comforting and full of flavor. Just like Kuromi's intimidating exterior, but inside she's as sweet as can be. To make this distinctive squash even better, it is stuffed with a savory filling of rice and pork—the ultimate fall weather feast.

FOR THE KABOCHA

- 1 (2-pound) whole kabocha squash
- 2 tablespoons olive oil
- 1 teaspoon kosher salt
- ½ teaspoon ground black pepper

FOR THE FILLING

- ½ cup sliced dried shiitake mushrooms
- 2 cups hot water, for soaking
- 1 tablespoon olive oil
- 2 garlic cloves, minced
- 1 medium shallot, minced
- 8 ounce ground pork
- 1 teaspoon peeled, grated fresh ginger
- 1 cup cooked short-grain rice
- 3 tablespoons tamari
- 1 tablespoon mirin
- 1 tablespoon honey
- ½ teaspoon sesame oil

To make the kabocha: Rinse and dry the kabocha. Use a sharp knife to cut around the top, as you would a pumpkin. Pull off the "lid" and set it aside. Use a spoon to scrape out and discard the seeds and fibrous pulp. Rub the kabocha, inside and outside, with the olive oil and sprinkle with the salt and pepper.

Preheat the oven to 400°F. Grease an 8 by 8-inch baking dish with nonstick cooking spray.

For the mushrooms: In a medium bowl, add the shiitake mushrooms and hot water. Set aside.

To make the filling: In a large skillet over medium-high heat, heat the olive oil. Add the garlic and shallot and cook until softened, 2 to 3 minutes.

Add the ground pork and ginger. Cook until the pork is no longer pink, 6 to 8 minutes.

Drain the shiitake mushrooms.

Add the cooked rice and shiitake mushrooms to the skillet and cook until fragrant, 2 to 3 minutes.

Stir in the tamari, mirin, honey, and sesame oil.

Place the kabocha in the prepared baking dish and stuff the squash with the filling. Replace the stemmed lid. Cover the kabocha with aluminum foil.

Bake for 1 hour. Reduce the oven temperature to 350°F. Remove the foil and bake the kabocha until soft, about 30 minutes.

Slice to serve.

Cinnamoroll Cottage Pie

MAKES **10** SERVINGS

Thanks to his fluffy ears, Cinnamoroll can fly around and look for adventures. The sky is his highway, but this cottage pie will always bring him back down to Earth. The mashed potatoes topping this tasty casserole look just like the soft, fluffy clouds he's used to flying through. This pie is filled with savory simmered beef and vegetables, making this hearty dish a complete meal after a day of flying.

FOR THE MASHED POTATOES

3 russet potatoes, peeled and quartered

⅔ cup whole milk

4 tablespoons unsalted butter

2 tablespoons grated parmesan cheese

1 teaspoon seasoned salt

¼ teaspoon ground black pepper

FOR THE FILLING

2 tablespoons olive oil

1 medium onion, diced

2 medium carrots, diced

2 celery stalks, diced

8 ounces white mushrooms, quartered

2 garlic cloves, minced

1½ pounds ground beef

1 tablespoon Worcestershire sauce

2 tablespoons tomato paste

1½ teaspoons ground oregano

1½ teaspoons dried rosemary

1½ teaspoons dried thyme

½ teaspoon kosher salt

¼ teaspoon ground black pepper

1 cup red wine

½ cup frozen peas

3 tablespoons grated cheddar cheese

2 tablespoons unsalted butter, cubed

To make the mashed potatoes: In a large pot, combine the potatoes with enough water to cover by 1 inch. Place the pot over high heat, bring to a boil, then reduce the heat to maintain a simmer and cook until tender, 15 minutes. Drain but do not rinse the potatoes. Return the potatoes to the pot and mash together with the milk and butter. Stir in the parmesan. Season with the seasoned salt and pepper. Set aside.

Preheat the oven to 375°F.

To make the filling: In a large ovenproof skillet over medium-high heat, heat the olive oil. Add the onion, carrots, celery, mushrooms, and garlic. Cook until softened, 10 minutes.

Add the ground beef and cook until no longer pink, 4 to 5 minutes. Stir in the Worcestershire sauce, tomato paste, oregano, rosemary, thyme, kosher salt, and pepper.

Stir in the wine and the peas. Simmer until slightly thickened, 5 minutes.

Top with the mashed potatoes, leaving space around the edges. Sprinkle with the cheddar and dot with the butter cubes.

Bake until browned, 20 minutes.
Let cool slightly and serve.

CHAPTER FOUR

Kawaii Desserts

"Save room for dessert" isn't just a saying, it's a lifestyle. A lot of Hello Kitty's friends happen to have sugary names related to their favorite confections. Cinnamoroll is named after his cinnamon roll-like tail. Chococat's little cherub nose is inspired by chocolate chips. How lucky to be named after such sweet snacks.

Perhaps desserts are so indulgent because of the time and effort it takes to make them. Pompompurin's favorite cream caramel puddings (see page 83) are a labor of love. It takes patience to make the caramel and the pudding. While the waiting might be the hardest part, the satisfying plop of the pudd makes it all worth it. It's the same with churros (see page 81); Cinnamoroll loves them, and they take a fair amount of time to make. But the huge payoff is the cinnamon sugary goodness that can't be beat.

Japanese desserts are slightly less sweet, but unique in flavor. Kuromi Sweet Sesame Mochi (page 85) is filled with a black sesame paste that is decidedly different from Western desserts, but the pink and black colors of

Kuromi will keep you interested. Candied strawberries (see page 89) are a dessert as dapper as Tuxedosam. A popular street food dessert, once you break through the glazed candy shell, the fruit really shines.

Sometimes you just crave a traditional dessert. Chococat knows his way around a chocolate chip, and when it comes to good old-fashioned chocolate chip cookies (see page 72), there's nothing quite as satisfying. Some recipes are memorable because of who made them. Hello Kitty adores her mom's pie—Mary White's Apple Pie (page 73)—because it's made with love. The sweet apples and pastry are the perfect pair, just like Hello Kitty and her mama.

Pochacco Banana Ice Cream

If there's one thing Pochacco can't resist, it's banana ice cream. Sweet, refreshing, and dairy-free, it's a great treat to indulge in without hesitation. It's so simple to make, Pochacco can make it right before he goes out for a walk in Fuwafuwa Town, and when he returns, the cool, creamy concoction will be ready to enjoy.

3 large bananas, peeled, sliced, and frozen

¼ cup oat milk

½ teaspoon vanilla extract

¼ teaspoon ground cinnamon

¼ teaspoon kosher salt

¼ cup chopped dark chocolate, plus more for garnish

In a blender, combine the frozen bananas, oat milk, vanilla, cinnamon, and salt. Blend until creamy. Transfer to a freezer-safe sealable container.

Fold in the chopped chocolate.

Freeze until solid, 2 hours.

Scoop to serve, and top with more chopped chocolate for garnish.

Pochacco loves to have fun, which means even his favorite dessert can be changed up for some added excitement. Banana ice cream is a good base to start, but add bits of chopped fruit and nuts for a healthy vibe. Or go crazy and plus it up with cocoa powder and peanut butter to make it rich and refined. You can even use banana ice cream to make an energizing smoothie, something Pochacco would love after a full day of playing sports.

Chococat Chocolate Chip Cookies

MAKES **32** COOKIES

Chococat got his name because of his little chocolate-colored nose. He may have antenna-like whiskers, but with a nose like that, he can surely smell chocolate chip cookies baking from a mile away. These cookies are crispy on the outside and chewy on the inside, just as perfect as Chococat's little nose.

3 cups all-purpose flour

1 teaspoon baking soda

½ teaspoon kosher salt

1 cup (2 sticks) unsalted butter, at room temperature

1 cup packed light brown sugar

½ cup granulated sugar

1 tablespoon molasses

1 teaspoon vanilla extract

2 large eggs

2 cups large dark chocolate chips

In a large bowl, whisk the flour, baking soda, and salt to combine. Set aside.

In the bowl of a stand mixer fitted with the paddle attachment (or in a large bowl with a handheld mixer), cream the butter, brown sugar, and granulated sugar on medium speed until fluffy, 4 to 5 minutes.

Stir in the molasses and vanilla.

One at a time, add the eggs until just combined.

Slowly add the flour mixture, stirring until just combined.

Fold in the chocolate chips.

Cover and refrigerate the dough for 1 hour.

Preheat the oven to 350°F. Line two baking sheets with parchment paper.

For each cookie, drop 2 tablespoons of dough onto the prepared baking sheets, making 32 rounds.

Bake both sheets until browned, 12 to 14 minutes. Let cool for 5 minutes on the baking sheets, then transfer to a wire rack.

Mary White's Apple Pie

MAKES **8** SERVINGS

Hello Kitty loves her mama, Mary White. Mary takes good care of her family and often wears an apron so she can bake special things, like Hello Kitty's favorite apple pie. The fruit is such a big part of Kitty's life that she describes herself as five apples tall and weighing as much as three apples. The perfect amount to make a full pie, which is delicious served with a nice big scoop of Pochacco Banana Ice Cream (page 71).

FOR THE CRUST

2½ cups all-purpose flour, plus more for dusting

2 teaspoons granulated sugar

½ teaspoon ground cinnamon

½ teaspoon kosher salt

1 cup (2 sticks) unsalted butter, cold and cubed

8 to 10 tablespoons ice water

FOR THE PIE

8 small Granny Smith apples, peeled, cored, and thinly sliced

1 tablespoon fresh lemon juice

2 tablespoons cornstarch

½ cup (1 stick) unsalted butter, melted

½ cup packed light brown sugar

½ cup granulated sugar

2 teaspoons vanilla extract

1 teaspoon ground cinnamon

½ teaspoon ground nutmeg

¼ teaspoon ground cloves

¼ teaspoon kosher salt

FOR THE EGG WASH

1 large egg

1 tablespoon water

To make the crust: In a large bowl, whisk the flour, granulated sugar, cinnamon, and salt to combine. With a pastry cutter, cut the cold butter into the flour mixture, until crumbly.

One tablespoon at a time, stir in the ice water until the dough just comes together. Divide the dough in half and pat it into disks. Wrap each disk in plastic wrap and refrigerate for 30 minutes.

To make the pie: In a medium bowl, toss the apples with the lemon juice. Sprinkle the cornstarch over the apples and set aside.

In a small bowl, stir together the melted butter, brown sugar, granulated sugar, vanilla, cinnamon, nutmeg, cloves, and salt.

Continues on next page

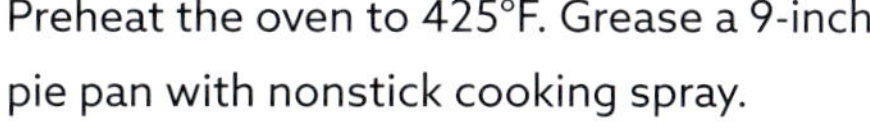

Preheat the oven to 425°F. Grease a 9-inch pie pan with nonstick cooking spray.

Dust a work surface lightly with flour. Unwrap one of the dough disks, place it on the floured surface, and roll it into a 13-inch circle. Transfer to the prepared pie pan, pressing the crust into the bottom and up the sides of the pan.

Layer the apples in the crust and cover with the sugar mixture.

Roll the remaining dough disk into a 12-inch circle, then cut the dough into ten equal strips. Lay five strips across the pie vertically, spaced equally. Pull back every other vertical strip, then lay one of the strips horizontally across the pie, close to the folded-back vertical strips. Fold down the vertical strips, pulling back the other strips, and lay down the second horizontal strip. Repeat the process, weaving the strips up and back until all the strips have been used.

Trim the excess overhanging dough, pinching the edges closed. With the excess dough, create a small bow and place into the upper corner of the pie.

To make the egg wash: In a small bowl, whisk the egg and water to blend. Use a pastry brush to brush the lattice and bow with egg wash. Place the pie onto a baking sheet.

Bake for 15 minutes.

Reduce the oven temperature to 350°F. Bake until fragrant and the crust is browned, 40 minutes more.

Let cool completely. Cut the pie into slices to serve.

Badtz-maru 'Nana Bread

MAKES
8
SERVINGS

Badtz-maru loves attracting attention. His mischievous attitude is the inspiration to make things feel a little extra, a little over the top, like this banana bread. A little bit of cocoa powder, some chocolate chips, and suddenly your average banana bread is rich and irresistible, just like Badtz-maru himself.

- 1⅔ cups all-purpose flour
- ½ cup Dutch-processed cocoa powder
- ½ cup packed light brown sugar
- ¼ cup granulated sugar
- 1 teaspoon baking soda
- ½ teaspoon ground cinnamon
- ¼ teaspoon kosher salt
- 3 ripe medium bananas, mashed
- ½ cup (1 stick) unsalted butter, melted
- 2 large eggs, lightly beaten
- ½ teaspoon vanilla extract
- 1 cup semisweet chocolate chips

Preheat the oven to 350°F. Line a 9 by 5-inch loaf pan with parchment paper and grease the parchment with nonstick cooking spray.

In a large bowl, whisk the flour, cocoa powder, brown sugar, granulated sugar, baking soda, cinnamon, and salt to combine. Make a well in the center of the dry ingredients.

Stir in the bananas, melted butter, eggs, and vanilla. Stir in the chocolate chips. Pour the batter into the prepared pan and smooth the top.

Bake until golden brown and an instant-read thermometer reads 200°F, about 1 hour.

Let cool for 10 minutes, then transfer to a wire rack to cool completely.

Cut into slices to serve.

My Melody Almond Pound Cake

Family is important to My Melody. Her iconic hood was made for her by her grandmother, and she never takes it off. Special moments with your family mean making the most of your time spent together, enjoying each other's company, and sharing a meal. My Melody's favorite dessert is almond pound cake. This large Bundt cake is big enough to share and would make a beautiful centerpiece for a picnic or a party at home with friends and family.

FOR THE CAKE

3 cups all-purpose flour

½ teaspoon baking soda

½ teaspoon kosher salt

1 cup (2 sticks) unsalted butter, at room temperature

8 ounces cream cheese, at room temperature

3 cups granulated sugar

6 large eggs

1½ teaspoons almond extract

FOR THE TOPPING

1½ cups powdered sugar

2 tablespoons unsalted butter, melted

1 teaspoon almond extract

2 tablespoons whole milk

¼ cup sliced almonds

Preheat the oven to 350°F. Grease a 10-inch Bundt cake pan with nonstick cooking spray.

To make the cake: In a large bowl whisk the flour, baking soda, and salt to combine. Set aside.

In the bowl of a stand mixer fitted with the paddle attachment (or in a large bowl with a handheld mixer), beat the butter and cream cheese on medium speed until creamy and smooth, 3 to 4 minutes. Add the granulated sugar and mix until just combined.

One at a time, mix in the eggs until combined, then mix in the almond extract.

Reduce the speed to low and gradually mix in the flour mixture, until just combined. Spoon the batter into the prepared pan. Tap the pan on the counter lightly to reduce the air bubbles. Place the filled Bundt pan on a baking sheet.

Bake the cake until golden and an instant-read thermometer reads 200°F, 1 hour. Transfer the cake to a wire rack and let cool completely.

Continues on next page

Gently turn the cake pan onto the wire rack, releasing the cake from the pan.

To make the topping: In a small bowl, whisk the powdered sugar, melted butter, and almond extract to combine.

One tablespoon at a time, stir in the milk until smooth and combined. Drizzle the icing over the cake. Sprinkle with the almonds.

Cut into slices to serve.

Donut Pond Donuts

MAKES **12** DONUTS

As a triplet with his sister, Pikki, and brother, Koroppi, Keroppi knows sharing is important. These donuts are named after their hometown of Donut Pond. Fluffy and sweet, the blue pond and little lily pads are represented as an ode to the special times they share having adventures around the pond.

FOR THE DONUTS

1 cup all-purpose flour

1 cup cake flour

1 cup granulated sugar

2 teaspoons baking powder

½ teaspoon kosher salt

¼ teaspoon ground nutmeg

1½ cups buttermilk

2 large eggs, lightly beaten

1 teaspoon vanilla extract

2 tablespoons unsalted butter, melted

FOR THE ICING

2 cups powdered sugar

1½ tablespoons whole milk

½ teaspoon vanilla extract

1 or 2 drops light blue food coloring

2 drops green food coloring

3 ounces green fondant, for decorating

2 ounces pink fondant, for decorating

Preheat the oven to 400°F. Grease two donut pans (12 donuts total) with nonstick cooking spray.

To make the donuts: In a large bowl, whisk the all-purpose flour, cake flour, granulated sugar, baking powder, salt, and nutmeg to combine. Make a well in the center of the dry ingredients.

Stir in the buttermilk, eggs, and vanilla, until just combined. Stir in the melted butter. Transfer the batter to a piping bag and pipe the batter into the prepared pans.

Bake each pan until golden brown, 8 to 10 minutes. Transfer to a wire rack to cool.

To make the icing: In a medium bowl, whisk the powdered sugar, milk, and vanilla until smooth and combined. Divide the icing between two bowls.

Dye one bowl blue, stirring in the blue food coloring. Dye the other green, stirring in the green food coloring.

Continues on next page

Dip one half of each donut into the blue icing and let it dry on a wire rack for 10 minutes. Then dip the other half of each donut into the green icing and let it dry on the wire rack for another 10 minutes.

To decorate: When the icings are dry, cut small lily pads out of the green fondant and place onto the donuts.

Create small flowers from the pink fondant and place one on each lily pad.

Cinnamoroll Churros

MAKES **12** SERVINGS

Cinnamoroll was given his name because his little tail curls up just like a cinnamon roll. This pup with a cute name calls for cute treats loaded with cinnamon flavor. These churros are fried to a crispy texture and dipped in a sugary coating. They're so good they will keep your tail wagging for more.

1 cup water

2 tablespoons granulated sugar, plus ½ cup

2 tablespoons unsalted butter

1 teaspoon vanilla extract

¼ teaspoon kosher salt

1 cup all-purpose flour, sifted

1 large egg, beaten

¼ teaspoon ground nutmeg

4 cups vegetable oil

1 tablespoon ground cinnamon

In a medium saucepan over medium-high heat, combine the water, 2 tablespoons of the sugar, butter, vanilla, and salt. Bring to a boil.

Rapidly stir in the flour, until just combined. Remove from the heat.

Stir in the egg and nutmeg, until smooth. Spoon the dough into a pastry bag fitted with a star tip.

In a large Dutch oven over medium heat, heat the oil to 350°F.

Cut parchment paper into twelve 6-inch squares.

Pipe the dough into a spiral directly onto the parchment squares.

Carefully drop the churros (parchment and all) directly into the hot oil; use tongs to remove and discard the parchment. Cook until golden brown, 2 to 3 minutes. Transfer to a wire rack to drain.

In a shallow dish, whisk the remaining ½ cup sugar and cinnamon to combine.

Dip the hot churros into the cinnamon sugar mixture to serve.

Hangyodon Gelatin Cheesecake

MAKES **24** SERVINGS

Hangyodon has a special place in his heart for the sea. That goes for how his desserts look, too. These little glowy cubes look like the ocean on the top thanks to a jiggly blue gelatin, and have a smooth cream cheese filling with a sandy bottom layer that looks just like the beach—a yummy treat that is a reminder of Hangyodon's favorite place.

FOR THE CRUST

2 cups graham cracker crumbs

3 tablespoons packed light brown sugar

½ teaspoon ground cinnamon

¼ teaspoon kosher salt

½ cup (1 stick) unsalted butter, melted

FOR THE CREAM CHEESE LAYER

8 ounces cream cheese, at room temperature

½ cup powdered sugar

1 teaspoon fresh lime juice

½ teaspoon vanilla extract

1 (8-ounce) container frozen whipped topping, thawed

FOR THE GELATIN LAYER

1 (6-ounce) package blue raspberry gelatin

3 cups boiling water

Preheat the oven to 350°F.

To make the crust: In a medium bowl, whisk the graham cracker crumbs, brown sugar, cinnamon, and salt to combine. Stir in the melted butter until combined. Press the mixture into a 9 by 13-inch baking dish. Bake for 15 minutes. Remove and set aside to cool completely.

To make the cream cheese layer: In the bowl of a stand mixer fitted with the paddle attachment (or in a large bowl with a handheld mixer), beat the cream cheese, powdered sugar, lime juice, and vanilla on medium speed until smooth, 3 to 5 minutes.

Fold in the whipped topping, until just combined. Evenly spread the cream cheese mixture onto the graham cracker crust. Refrigerate for 30 minutes.

To make the gelatin layer: In a large heatproof bowl, whisk the gelatin and boiling water until the gelatin dissolves, 2 to 3 minutes. Set aside to cool, 30 minutes.

Carefully pour the cooled gelatin over the cream cheese layer. Refrigerate until the gelatin has set, 8 hours or overnight.

Cut into squares to serve.

Pompompurin Cream Caramel Puddings

MAKES **4** SERVINGS

Pompompurin likes to enjoy foods that are just like him—soft and squishy! These melt-in-your-mouth cream caramel puddings are a special dessert you can enjoy any time. The best part is plopping them out and watching them jiggle!

FOR THE CARAMEL

½ cup granulated sugar

¼ cup water

FOR THE CUSTARD

1½ cups whole milk

3 large eggs

⅓ cup granulated sugar

1 teaspoon vanilla extract

⅛ teaspoon kosher salt

4 cups boiling water

Grease four 5-inch ramekins with nonstick cooking spray. Set aside.

To make the caramel: In a small saucepan over medium heat, combine the sugar and water. Do not stir. Let cook. The sugar water will turn into liquid, then start bubbling. Watch the color: When it becomes a deep brown, immediately pour the caramel evenly into the prepared ramekins. Set aside.

Preheat the oven to 350°F. Set aside a medium roasting pan with 3-inch-high sides.

To make the custard: In a medium saucepan over medium low heat, bring the milk to a low simmer. Cook until lightly bubbling around the edges and an instant-read thermometer reads 125°F, 5 to 8 minutes. Turn off the heat.

In a large bowl, whisk the eggs, sugar, vanilla, and salt to blend.

Slowly add a ladle of the warm milk to the eggs, whisking to temper. Add a second ladleful, still whisking. Finally, whisk in the remaining warm milk.

Strain the custard through a fine-mesh sieve set over another bowl.

Continues on next page

Evenly pour or ladle the custard into the ramekins, over the caramel. Place the ramekins into the baking dish. Pour the boiling water into the baking dish so the water comes halfway up the sides of the ramekins.

Bake until just set, 35 to 40 minutes.

Use tongs to carefully remove the ramekins from the hot water. Let cool completely.

Cover each ramekin with plastic wrap and refrigerate overnight.

Run a sharp knife around the inside of each ramekin. Invert the custard onto a dish to serve.

Kuromi Sweet Sesame Mochi

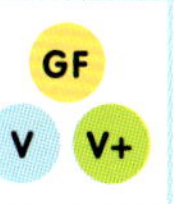

What makes Kuromi an icon is her sense of style—the jester hat, the twinkle in her eye, and most of all, the pink-and-black color combo she embraces in her own unique way. Like her fashion, this mochi takes those two colors and makes them edible. Soft pink mochi encases luscious black sesame filling—a tasty treat for the Kuromi in us all.

FOR THE FILLING

⅓ cup black sesame seeds

2 tablespoons granulated sugar

½ teaspoon coconut oil

FOR THE MOCHI

¾ cup mochiko (sweet rice flour)

¾ cup water

¼ cup granulated sugar

1 drop pink food coloring

½ cup potato starch

To make the filling: In a small skillet over medium heat, toast the sesame seeds until fragrant, 2 to 3 minutes. Transfer to a mini food processor, add the sugar, and pulse until finely ground. Add the coconut oil and continue to pulse until thickened. Form the filling into six equal balls. Refrigerate until ready to use.

To make the mochi: In a microwave-safe bowl, stir together the mochiko, water, sugar, and pink food coloring until smooth. Cover the bowl with plastic wrap and microwave on high power for 1 minute. Stir well.

Return the bowl to the microwave and cook for another 1½ minutes, stopping to stir every 30 seconds, until stretchy.

Sift ¼ cup of the potato starch onto a clean surface. Carefully scoop the cooked mochi onto the potato starch. Sift the remaining potato starch on top. Cut the mochi into six equal pieces.

Continues on next page

Take one piece and shake off the excess potato starch, form it into a flat circle, and place a sesame ball in the center. Pull up the edges of the mochi and pinch them together to close the mochi around the sesame ball. Place the ball, seam-side down, on a serving dish. Repeat with the remaining mochi and sesame balls.

Kuromi may have the personality of a tomboy, but it's her girly side that makes her want to lean into supercute sweets. The filling in these sweet mochi may be black sesame to match Kuromi's hood, but the flavor can be easily changed with a variety of alternatives. Try filling these with a hazelnut spread for a super sweet bite. Or enjoy a traditional Japanese red bean filling; it's the perfect little snack to have with afternoon tea. If you prefer more texture, crunchy peanut butter will do the trick. The combination of stretchy mochi and peanut butter is out of this world. Try a bunch of different options and get adventurous with your food!

LittleTwinStars' Cupcakes

MAKES **18** CUPCAKES

Kiki and Lala love each other's company. The two were born on Christmas Eve and do everything together, so a paired dessert just makes sense. These cupcakes are pink for Lala and blue for Kiki, and even look just like the twins themselves. Filled with tangy lemon curd, these tasty treats will have you dreaming of the stars.

FOR THE CUPCAKES

2½ cups sifted cake flour

2 teaspoons baking powder

¼ teaspoon kosher salt

¾ cup (1½ sticks) unsalted butter

1¾ cups granulated sugar

3 large eggs

1 teaspoon vanilla extract

1 cup buttermilk

Pink food coloring, for tinting

Light blue food coloring, for tinting

1¼ cups lemon curd

FOR THE FROSTING

1 cup (2 sticks) unsalted butter, at room temperature

3 cups powdered sugar

1 teaspoon vanilla extract

¼ teaspoon kosher salt

¼ cup heavy cream

12 ounces pink fondant, for decorating

12 ounces light blue fondant, for decorating

2 ounces black fondant, for decorating

Preheat the oven to 350°F. Line two cupcake pans with liners.

To make the cupcakes: In a medium bowl, whisk the flour, baking powder, and salt to combine. Set aside.

In the bowl of a stand mixer fitted with the paddle attachment (or in a large bowl with a handheld mixer), cream the butter and granulated sugar until fluffy, 3 to 4 minutes.

Stir in the eggs and vanilla, until just combined.

In 3 additions, alternate adding the buttermilk and the dry ingredients, stirring, until just combined. Divide the batter equally between two bowls.

Use the pink food coloring to dye the first bowl of batter, stirring until incorporated. Spoon the pink batter into half of the prepared cupcake wells, dividing it evenly.

Use the light blue food coloring to dye the second bowl of batter, stirring until incorporated. Spoon the blue batter into the remaining wells, dividing it evenly.

Bake until just done and an inserted toothpick comes out clean, 15 to 17 minutes.

Continues on next page

Transfer to a wire rack to cool.

Use a spoon to core out 1 tablespoon of cake from the center of each cupcake. Fill the hole with lemon curd.

To make the frosting: In a large bowl with a handheld mixer, mix the butter, powdered sugar, vanilla, and salt on low speed, until combined. Slowly pour in the cream and beat on medium speed until light and fluffy, 2 minutes.

Frost the cupcakes, using an offset spatula to create a flat top.

To decorate: Roll the pink fondant to ⅛ inch thick. Use clean kitchen scissors and scallop-edge scissors to cut out Lala's hair, then place on half the cupcakes. Do the same with the light blue fondant for Kiki's hair.

Use small pieces of black fondant to create their eyes and mouths to complete the cupcakes.

Serve.

Tuxedosam Candied Strawberries

MAKES **8** SERVINGS

When you're a dapper penguin like Tuxedosam, having extra bow ties on hand is a must—you never know when a friend might need one. Or if you have an emergency formal ceremony, you can never be too prepared. Take Tuxedosam's lead and make these skewered candied strawberries. Sweet and crunchy, the pop of fresh fruit is very refreshing. Now you can hand out bow tie–shaped fruit at your leisure.

16 fresh strawberries, washed, dried, and hulled

8 fresh blueberries

2 cups granulated sugar

¼ cup water

¼ cup light corn syrup

8 (6-inch) skewers

Line a baking sheet with parchment paper. Set aside.

Skewer 1 strawberry through the hulled side, 1 blueberry, and another strawberry through the pointed end to form a bow tie. Repeat with the remaining fruit to create eight skewered fruit bow ties.

In a small saucepan over medium-high heat, combine the sugar, water, and corn syrup. Bring to a simmer and cook until a candy thermometer reaches the hard crack stage, 300°F. Remove from the heat.

Dip the skewers into the syrup, letting the excess drip off into the pan. Place the skewers on the prepared baking sheet to harden, 1 to 2 minutes.

Serve.

CHAPTER FIVE

Fanciful Drinks

A good beverage can be enjoyed any time of day. Hello Kitty and her friends can meet up and quench their thirst mid-afternoon, or they can sip on a beverage with a good meal. Drinks not only keep up your hydration, but when shared with friends, they also keep your conversation going. A few sips while conversing with friends can be incredibly therapeutic and help keep your spirits high.

Fruit-based drinks are a charming choice and always refreshing. LittleTwinStars Kiki and Lala know star shapes make everything more magical and that is for certain when it comes to starfruit juice (see page 98), a citrus beverage that tastes as enchanting as it looks. Pompompurin might partake in an invigorating watermelon cooler (see page 103) after a long day of taking walks—and naps.

Hello Kitty knows accessories enhance your style—just look at her iconic red bow. In the same manner, Kuromi's jester hat and Chococat's collar are their signature statement pieces. The black sesame boba (see page 106) and hot cocoa (see page 99) each has its own adornment—a whipped cream cheese topping that finishes the drinks perfectly.

Every social gathering needs a good thirst-quencher. The cream soda float (see page 97) is as sparkling as Tuxedosam's attire and an impressive sip to share with friends at a get-together. For a larger gathering, multiple glasses of Pond Party Punch (page 96) are a festive way to enhance a day of boomerang around Donut Pond with friends and family. Plus, it's a drink and dessert all in one!

Staying hydrated and appreciating those closest to you can create the best memories. Raising a glass of punch or a warm beverage to cheer a pal is the best feeling that will also replenish your energy and keep your spirits lifted.

Hello Boba

MAKES 1 SERVING

One of Hello Kitty's favorite things to do is hang out with her friends, whether doing crafts, riding bikes, or heading to the nearest cafe for boba. This popular milk tea is special because it's made with one of Hello Kitty's favorite ingredients—bright red strawberries—which help make this drink the perfect shade of pink. Poured over chewy boba, it's a great afternoon pick-me-up.

FOR THE MILK

½ cup water

¼ cup diced strawberries, plus 2 slices for garnish

1½ tablespoons granulated sugar

¾ cup oat milk

FOR THE TEA

½ cup boiling water

1 black tea bag

FOR THE BOBA SIMPLE SYRUP

1 cup water

1 cup packed light brown sugar

¼ teaspoon vanilla extract

FOR THE BOBA

5 cups water

¼ cup boba pearls

To make the milk: In a small saucepan over low heat, combine the water, diced strawberries, and granulated sugar. Simmer until thick, 4 to 5 minutes. Remove from the heat and let cool slightly.

Press the mixture through a fine-mesh sieve set over a bowl to remove the seeds. Let cool completely. Transfer to a medium container and add the milk. Refrigerate until ready to use.

To make the tea: In a mug, combine the boiling water and tea bag. Steep for 5 minutes. Remove and discard the tea bag. Let cool completely. Refrigerate until ready to use.

To make the boba simple syrup: In a small saucepan over high heat, bring the water and the brown sugar to a boil, until the sugar dissolves, 2 minutes. Let cool. Stir in the vanilla and set aside.

To make the boba: In a large saucepan over high heat, bring the water to a boil. Add the boba pearls, turn down the heat to maintain a simmer, and cook until softened, 25 minutes.

Continues on next page

Turn off the heat. Cover the saucepan and let sit for another 25 minutes.

Drain and rinse the boba pearls, then pour them into the cooled simple syrup. Let soak for 30 minutes.

Scoop the boba into a tall glass.
Add 1 cup of ice. Pour in the cooled black tea.

Finally, pour in the strawberry milk.

Place the strawberry slices on top to serve.

The best thing about recipes is being able to mix and match things to create perfect pairings. Invite friends over and have them bring the food while you provide the drinks. Should Hello Kitty want some company, she can invite Pochacco to bring fruit sando (see page 33) to go with this fruit-based drink. Or maybe My Melody can bring some of her famous almond pound cake (see page 77) to go with hot tea. Pairing food and drinks is just like pairing friends and fun—the two go together to form the ultimate combination, and the possibilities of new friends and new foods are endless.

Pond Party Punch

The best part about living at Donut Pond are the summer parties with friends. When Keroppi has a get-together, there's always a lot of food and fun. His big family is the life of the party. This fizzy party punch is great poolside because it's cooled with a whole ice pop, placed right in the cup! A snack and a drink all in one? It's the ideal party refreshment.

2 tablespoons green apple syrup

1½ cups lemon-lime soda

1 raspberry ice pop

2 tablespoons fresh raspberries

1 lime slice

In a tall glass, combine the green apple syrup and lemon-lime soda. Stir well.

Add ice, the raspberry ice pop, and fresh raspberries.

Garnish with the lime slice to serve.

Tuxedosam Cream Soda Float

MAKES 1 SERVING

Tuxedosam is all about sophisticated charm. Just look at his bow tie collection—one for every day of the year. His dapper attitude goes for his taste in food and beverages, too. This sparkling drink emulates Tuxedosam's colors, from his fashionable blue and white colorway to his cheeky red bow tie. An elegant drink for a stylish penguin with exquisite fashion sense.

3 tablespoons blue raspberry syrup
1 teaspoon fresh lime juice
1 cup lemon-lime soda
2 tablespoons heavy cream
2 maraschino cherries

Fill a tall glass with ice. Pour in the blue raspberry syrup, lime juice, and lemon-lime soda. Stir well. Add ice.

Pour in the heavy cream.

Skewer the cherries to form a bow tie and place on top of the glass to serve.

LittleTwinStars' Starfruit Juice

Kiki and Lala want to become the best stars they can be, and they love spreading joy and happiness. Star-shaped things are their personal insignia, and that includes what they eat and drink. This chilled fruit juice is refreshing on a spring day, and it's made even sweeter with the addition of celestial-shaped fruit.

4 cups ginger ale, chilled

2 cups sparkling water, chilled

½ cup fresh grapefruit juice

½ cup pineapple juice

2 teaspoons fresh lemon juice

2 starfruits, washed, dried, and sliced

Into a large pitcher, combine the ginger ale, sparkling water, grapefruit juice, pineapple juice, and lemon juice. Stir well.

Add half of the sliced starfruit, reserving the other half for garnish.

To serve, fill a tall glass with ice. Pour in the juice. Garnish with one of the reserved starfruit slices.

Chocococat Hot Cocoa

Chococat loves his sweets, and sometimes a drink can become a dessert, especially when it's a warm mug of luxurious hot chocolate. This is no ordinary cup of cocoa but rather a spin on a classic thick French hot chocolate. To make this treat even more special, it's topped with a whipped cream cheese foam and a light sprinkle of crushed chocolate cookies. Simply irresistible!

FOR THE CHOCOLATE

1 cup whole milk

¼ cup heavy cream

2 ounces dark chocolate, chopped

2 ounces semisweet chocolate, chopped

⅛ teaspoon vanilla extract

⅛ teaspoon kosher salt

FOR THE TOPPING

2 ounces cream cheese, at room temperature

2 tablespoons powdered sugar

2 tablespoons heavy cream

1 tablespoon crushed gluten-free chocolate cookies

To make the chocolate: In a medium saucepan over medium heat, combine the milk and heavy cream. Heat, whisking constantly, until warm, 2 to 3 minutes.

Turn off the heat and stir in the dark chocolate, semisweet chocolate, vanilla, and salt, until the chocolate has melted completely. Pour into a mug.

To make the topping: In a small bowl with a handheld mixer, mix the cream cheese, powdered sugar, and heavy cream until fluffy, 1 minute. Spoon onto the hot chocolate.

Sprinkle with the chocolate cookies to serve.

Continues on next page

Hot chocolate is the ultimate comfort drink. Customizing it with your personal touch makes it even better. Add some mint for a cool uplevel experience, or maybe a swirl of peanut butter for a thick, indulgent sip. Chococat loves chocolate, so imagine adding even more. Chocolate shavings, chocolate chips, chocolate syrup, all piled on top. That's a whole lot of chocolate, but the more the merrier.

Hangyodon Blue Lemonade

MAKES 1 SERVING

Hangyodon has a good sense of what tastes good to him, and it's usually sea water. At least this drink only looks like the ocean, and luckily it tastes much better. A creamy coconut lemonade will remind you of the beach, but it's the spectacle of the color change that will have you dreaming of the briny deep.

- **2 tablespoons granulated sugar**
- **2 tablespoons boiling water**
- **1 teaspoon butterfly pea flower tea powder**
- **¾ cup coconut milk**
- **¼ cup fresh lemon juice**

To make the simple syrup, in a small heatproof bowl, stir together the sugar and boiling water, until the sugar dissolves, about 1 to 2 minutes. Let cool completely.

In a tall glass, stir together the simple syrup, butterfly pea flower tea powder, and coconut milk. Add ice.

Stir in the lemon juice to watch the color change.

Cinnamoroll Horchata Freeze

MAKES 2 SERVINGS

After flying high in the sky, Cinnamoroll can cool off with a nice, refreshing drink. Made with horchata rice milk and vegan ice cream, this freeze is full of cinnamon flavor. Blended to make it extra thick and creamy, it's as light and airy as flying through fluffy clouds.

FOR THE HORCHATA

¼ cup uncooked white rice, washed

1 cup water

1 cinnamon stick

¾ cup almond milk

¼ cup granulated sugar

½ teaspoon vanilla extract

FOR THE DRINK

3 cups vegan oat milk ice cream

1 teaspoon ground cinnamon

½ teaspoon vanilla extract

¼ teaspoon ground nutmeg

To make the horchata: In a blender, combine the rice and water. Blend until the rice is finely ground, 2 to 3 minutes. Pour into an airtight container and add the cinnamon stick. Refrigerate for 8 hours or overnight.

Blend the horchata again, until smooth. Strain through a fine-mesh sieve into a serving pitcher and discard the residue.

Stir in the almond milk, sugar, and vanilla. Refrigerate until ready to use.

To make the drink: In a blender, combine the ice cream, 1 cup of the horchata, the ground cinnamon, and vanilla. Blend until smooth. Pour into two tall glasses.

Dust with nutmeg to garnish.

Pompompurin Watermelon Cooler

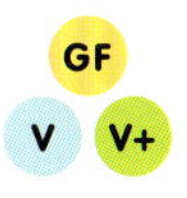

This cooler is light and invigorating thanks to ice-cold watermelon, sweet lychee, and sparkling soda. Like Pompompurin's beret, this is topped with its own flair—a mint sprig for freshness.

1 cup cubed watermelon, frozen

¼ cup lychees, peeled and pitted

1 tablespoon fresh lime juice

¾ cup lemon-lime soda, chilled

1 mint sprig

In a blender, combine the frozen watermelon, lychees, and lime juice. With the blender running, slowly pour in the lemon-lime soda. Blend until smooth. Pour into a tall glass.

Garnish with the mint sprig to serve.

Badtz-maru Green Tea Lemonade

When you eat as much sushi as Badtz-maru, you need to accompany it with a cleansing, restorative drink . . . so you can eat even more. This refreshing beverage combines two unique flavors—rich matcha and citrusy lemon—creating the perfect blend. A hint of yuzu adds just a touch of panache, satisfying even Badtz-maru's refined taste.

2 tablespoons granulated sugar

2 tablespoons boiling water

2 tablespoons warm water

1 tablespoon matcha powder

1 cup cold water

3 tablespoons fresh lemon juice

1 tablespoon yuzu juice

To make the simple syrup, in a small heatproof bowl, stir together the sugar and boiling water, until the sugar dissolves, about 1 to 2 minutes. Let cool completely.

In a small bowl, combine the warm water and matcha powder. Use a bamboo whisk to whisk, until smooth.

In a tall glass, pour in the matcha mixture, cold water, lemon juice, yuzu juice, and simple syrup. Stir well. Add ice to serve.

My Melody Raspberry Fizz

MAKES
1
SERVING

My Melody loves pink drinks because pink is her favorite color! It also matches the hood she wears every day when she's out around town. This color palette can be linked to a variety of fruits, but the most radiant one is the raspberry. Tart yet sweet, this fizzy drink is the epitome of a pink dream.

½ cup cranberry juice

½ cup sparkling water

¼ cup fresh orange juice

1 tablespoon fresh lime juice

2 tablespoons fresh raspberries

1 fresh mint leaf

Fill a large glass with ice. Pour in the cranberry juice, sparkling water, orange juice, and lime juice.

Add the raspberries and mint leaf to serve.

Kuromi Black Sesame Boba

MAKES 1 SERVING

Kuromi can be quite a character. Despite her outward appearance, she's actually very girly and enjoys writing in her diary and reading romance novels. This beverage is perfect for a relaxing day at home. The nutty and sweet flavors of the black sesame pair well with the chewy boba. Topped with a fluffy pink cream cheese, the colors are similar to Kuromi, and just as sweet.

FOR THE BOBA SIMPLE SYRUP

1 cup water

1 cup packed light brown sugar

¼ teaspoon vanilla extract

FOR THE BOBA

5 cups water

¼ cup boba pearls

FOR THE DRINK

½ cup whole milk

2 tablespoons ground black sesame seeds

FOR THE CREAM CHEESE TOPPING

2 ounces cream cheese, at room temperature

2 tablespoons powdered sugar

3 maraschino cherries

2 teaspoons maraschino cherry juice

2 tablespoons heavy cream

To make the boba simple syrup: In a small saucepan over high heat, bring the water and brown sugar to a boil, until the sugar dissolves, 2 minutes. Let cool. Stir in the vanilla and set aside.

To make the boba: In a large saucepan over high heat, bring the water to a boil. Add the boba pearls, turn down the heat to maintain a simmer, and cook until softened, 25 minutes. Turn off the heat. Cover the saucepan and let sit for another 25 minutes.

Drain and rinse the boba pearls, then pour them into the cooled simple syrup. Let soak for 30 minutes.

To make the drink: In a blender, combine the milk, sesame seeds, and 1 cup of ice. Blend until slushy, 30 seconds.

Scoop the boba into a tall glass and pour in the blended black sesame milk.

To make the topping: In a small bowl with a handheld mixer, mix the cream cheese, powdered sugar, cherries, cherry juice, and heavy cream until fluffy, 1 minute. Spoon onto the drink to serve.

Pochacco Carrot Juice

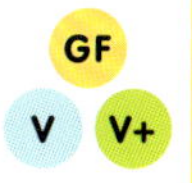

Fuwafuwa Town is filled with farm fields, making it the perfect place for Pochacco to indulge in one of his favorite foods—carrots! Carrots are great in salads and even better in cakes, but did you know you can also drink carrots? You need to blend them up first, of course, but it's worth the wait. They're good for you and give you an extra zing of energy. No wonder Pochacco is always on the go.

2 large carrots, peeled and cut into large chunks

1 tablespoon fresh lemon juice

1-inch piece fresh ginger

½ cup fresh orange juice

Fresh parsley, for garnish

In a blender, combine the carrots, lemon juice, and ginger. Blend until thick.

With the blender running, slowly pour in the orange juice, until the mixture thins out. Strain through a fine-mesh sieve set over a liquid measuring cup.

Fill a tall glass with ice and pour in the juice.

Garnish with the parsley to serve.

ACKNOWLEDGMENTS

As someone who has loved Sanrio characters my whole life, and whose first job was working in a Sanrio store as a teen, this book was a joy to work on. Thank you to my family, taste testers, and fellow Hello Kitty fans; Alice Kawakami, Kyle, Tyler, and Mason Fujikawa, AJ Camarillo, Mel Caylo, Lyn Cowan, Cheryl deCarvalho, Chrissy Dinh, Chrys Hasegawa, Sarah Kuhn, Robb Pearlman, Kim Trinh, and Mary Yogi. Special thanks to Jordana Hawkins, Mary Boyer, Syarlin Syafruddin, Amy Cianfrone, Kara Thornton, Running Press, and Sanrio.

Finally, to my kids: Always dream big.

INDEX

D